VGM Opportunities Series

OPPORTUNITIES IN
SPORTS MEDICINE
CAREERS

William Ray Heitzmann

Foreword by
Gabe Mirkin, M.D.
Associate Clinical Professor
Georgetown University School of Medicine

VGM Career Horizons
a division of *NTC Publishing Group*
Lincolnwood, Illinois USA

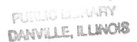

Cover Photo Credits:

Front cover: upper left, upper right, and lower left,
Sports Physical Therapists Inc; lower right, University
of Illinois at Chicago.

Back cover: upper left, American College of Traditional
Chinese Medicine; upper right, Elmhurst College; lower
left, New York Football Giants; lower right, Sports
Physical Therapists, Inc.

Library of Congress Cataloging-in-Publication Data

Heitzmann, William Ray.
    Opportunities in sports medicine / Wm. Ray Heitzmann.
      p.   cm. — (VGM opportunities series

    Includes bibliographical references.
    ISBN 0-8442-8168-9 (hardcover) : $12.95. — ISBN 0-8442-8169-7
(softcover) : $9.95
      1. Sports medicine—Vocational guidance. I. Title. II. Series.
    [DNLM: 1. Sports Medicine. 2. Vocational Guidance. QT 21 H473o]
RC1210.H475   1991
617.1'027—dc20
DNLM/DLC
for Library of Congress   91-27613
                                                    CIP

Published by VGM Career Horizons, a division of NTC Publishing Group.
© 1992 by NTC Publishing Group, 4255 West Touhy Avenue,
Lincolnwood (Chicago), Illinois 60646-1975 U.S.A.
Manufactured in the United States of America.

1 2 3 4 5 6 7 8 9 0 VP 9 8 7 6 5 4 3 2 1

ABOUT THE AUTHOR

Ray Heitzmann, Ph.D., Villanova University, has served as a teacher and coach of athletics in New Jersey, Pennsylvania, Illinois, and New York. At Thomas Jefferson University (Philadelphia), he taught in the College of Allied Health Sciences; his most recent coaching tenure was as head men's basketball coach at Neumann College (Pennsylvania).

Dr. Heitzmann has written numerous articles on sports, athletics, and sports medicine which have appeared in such publications as *Career World, Illinois Libraries, Catholic Library World, Coaching Clinic, Coach and Athlete, Education Age, PhillySport, The National Association of Basketball Coaches Bulletin, Philadelphia Inquirer, Catholic Standard and Times,* and others.

Following his undergraduate work at Villanova University, he obtained his master's degree at the University of Chicago and his doctorate at the University of Delaware. He took additional graduate work at Northwestern University and California State University at San Jose as well as some specialized courses at Orange County Community College (New York) and Triton Community College (Illinois).

ACKNOWLEDGMENTS

The author would like to thank the many players, coaches, and associated people who have contributed to his love and knowledge of sports. For their assistance in the preparation of this book, the author wishes to thank the following: Gabe Merkin, M.D., The Sports Medicine Institute, Silver Spring, MD, and associate clinical professor, Georgetown University School of Medicine; Robert Gallagher, M.S., coordinator YMCA–Delaware Valley cluster–Programs for Healthy Lifestyles, Lansdale, PA; Charlotte Rancilio, news services director, American Optometric Association; Ronnie Barnes, M.S., head athletic trainer, New York Giants (football); Joan Ingalls, Ed.D., sports psychologist and adjunct professor, William Patterson College, NJ; Michael Ranft, C.A., Hot Springs, Arkansas; Kevin Ergil, L.Ac., president, American College of Traditional Chinese Medicine, San Francisco; Larry Mathews, associate athletic director, Yale University; Hannah Bradford, American Association of Acupuncture and Oriental Medicine, Washington, DC; Gregory Boyle, L.Ac., Kansas City, MO, and public relations chair, American Association of Acupuncture and Oriental Medicine; Jack Miller, L.Ac., Pacific College of Oriental Medicine, San Diego, CA; Marnae Pearlman, administrative assistant, American College of Traditional Chinese Medicine, San Francisco; Vincent Di Stefano, M.D., The Graduate Hospital Human Performance and Sports Medicine Center, Wayne, PA; Andrew Clary, A.T.C., head athletic trainer, University of Miami; Art Hunter, Novo-Nordisk Medical Services; Joel Safly, A.T.C., Visalia (CA) Oaks minor league baseball team (Minnesota Twins); Linda Rowan, A.T.C., University of Hawaii at Hilo; Jose Bernal, The President's Health Club, Plano, TX; Kate Colliton and Bryna Vandergrift, Villanova University; Cindy Tumas, M.S., R.P.T., director, Southern Delaware Physical Therapy and Sports Institute; Raymond Pennacchia, V.P. marketing, Sports Physical Therapists, Wayne, PA; Nuala Carpenter, faculty member, Physical Therapist Assistant Program, Harcum College, Bryn Mawr, PA; Lori Warner, public relations coordinator, National Strength and Conditioning Association, Lincoln, NE; Richard Berenter, D.P.M., California College of Podiatric Medicine, podiatric director, St. Francis Hospital Center for Sports Medicine; Michael Billauer, D.C., Billauer Chiropractic Offices, team physician for men's U.S. Volleyball Olympic Team (1988); Pat Mosher, Ph.D., director, Human Performance Laboratory, University of Tennessee at Chattanooga; Marilee Matheny, M.S., director of fitness program, Shiley Sports and Health Center of Scripps Clinic, San Diego, CA; Richard Freccia, independent graphics producer/coordinator, statistician, stage manager, researcher college and professional sports, East Windsor, NJ; Michael Colgan, Ph.D., director, Colgan Institute, Encinitas, CA; Ann Grandjean, Ed.D., director, The International Center for Sports Nutrition, Omaha, NE; Bob Rotella, Ph.D., sports psychology specialist, University of Virginia; Betty Kelley, M.Ed., Sport Psychology Program, University of North Carolina at Greensboro; Neil Sherman, massage therapist, Chicago Health Club, Vernon Hills, IL; Bucky Grace, massage therapist, Penn Oaks Fitness and Tennis Club, West Chester, PA; D. Weight, professor, Department of Prosthetics and Orthotics, New York University; Andrew Myers, B.S., C.P.O., director, Prosthetic and Orthotic Services, West Hempstead, N.Y.; Kimberly Kumiega, director of communications, American Dental Association; Barbara Kratchman, director of communications, American Chiropractic Association; Page Elliott, supervisor accreditation programs, American Board for Certification in Orthotics and Prosthetics; Larry Shane, executive director, American Academy of Podiatric Sports Medicine; Jeffrey Krueger, director of communications and public relations, American College of Sports Medicine; Gary Delforge, Ed.D., University of Arizona; Philip J. Mayer, M.D., Department of Orthopedics, School of Medicine, State University of New York at Stony Brook; James Stacey, science news editor, American Medical Association; Jack Bell, assistant director, Division of Personal and Public Health Policy, American Medical Association; I. Lawrence Kerr, D.D.S., chairman, Committee on Dental Health and Committee on Drugs, United States Olympic Committee; Nancy Kelly, administrator, Good Samaritan Hospital, Long Island, N.Y.; Ronald Feingold, Ph.D., chairman, Department of Physical Education and Human Performance Science, Adelphia University (New York); John Steinbrink, Ed.D., Oklahoma State University; Kenneth Clarke, Ph.D., director, Sports Medicine Division, U.S. Olympic Committee; Ed Miersch, M.A., A.T.C., Sports Physical Therapists, Wayne, PA; Michael O'Shea, athletic trainer, University of Louisville; Stephanie Gately, women's basketball coach, St. Joseph's University (PA); Jim Corea, Ph.D., R.P.T., owner-manager Jim Corea's Gym, Cherry Hill, NJ and fitness/nutrition educator, Moorestown, NJ; Rick Wolff, editor, *The First Aider,* Cramer Products, Gardner, Kansas; Henry Nichols, Ed.D., director, basketball officials, NCAA; Don Casey, NBA assistant coach, Boston Celtics; Marty Walsh, sports official (umpire, referee), Newark, DE; Jill White, doctoral candidate, Exercise Physiology, University of Georgia; Gerry Kaplan, athletic director and basketball coach, O'Neil High School, Highland Falls, NY; Ed Kershner, Valley Forge Middle School, Valley Forge, PA; Ted Quedenfeld, administrative director,

Temple University Center for Sports Medicine and Science; Michael Sachs, University of Maryland Medical School; William Emper, M.D., sports orthopedist, Orthopedic Associates, Bryn Mawr, PA; Stephanie Cugini, Buena Athletic Club, Buena, NJ; Michele Sharp, women's basketball coach, Norwich University, Northfield, VT; Ortho Davis, executive director, National Athletic Trainers Association and athletic trainer, Philadelphia Eagles; Andy McGovern, director of intramurals and facilities, Villanova University; Larry Hanzel, athletic director (ret.), North Chicago High School; Bob Lambert, sports equipment manager, Villanova University; Dan Unger, A.T.C., head athletic trainer, Villanova University; Shelley Pennefather, Nippon Express Basketball Team, Japan; Liz Love, San Diego, CA; Peggy Melnick, Easton, PA; Richard Schoenberger, American Massage Therapy Association, Chicago; Larry Lester, Florida Institute of Traditional Chinese Medicine, St. Petersburg, FL.

A special thanks is made to Kathy, Rick, and Mary Heitzmann for their support as well as to Villanova University and the Ragdale Foundation, Lake Forest, Illinois, for their support during the preparation of this manuscript.

DEDICATION

Dedication of the book is made to my wonderful parents—Mary Tolland Heitzmann and William H. Heitzmann.

FOREWORD

It's fun to work with athletes. They are among the most highly motivated people in the world. To be successful, they have to demonstrate self-discipline and determination. When they are injured, they will do almost anything to help themselves heal quickly and return to their sports. The vast majority of injured athletes heal and continue to be in superb physical condition. Then you share in their future success on the playing field.

Athletes are treated by a team of professionals: doctors, osteopaths, nurses, trainers, podiatrists, exercise physiologists, coaches, physical therapists, occupational therapists, strength coaches, flexibility trainers, nutritionists, pharmacologists, and others. The type of treatment and the specific professional to administer the treatment are determined by the nature and extent of the injury.

Dr. Heitzmann has done an outstanding job in preparing this edition to help you search for your place in sports medicine. He has contacted the leading centers for training and listed them in an easy-to-read form. Read this book and find where you fit.

Gabe Mirkin, M.D.
Associate Clinical Professor
Georgetown University School of Medicine

Syndicated newspaper columnist,
television host, and fitness broadcaster.

CONTENTS

CHAPTER 1

SPORTS MEDICINE: AN INTRODUCTION

The explosion of interest in sports and growing participation in both men's and women's athletics worldwide has resulted in a concurrent growth in the profession of sports medicine and related careers. A dramatic shift in emphasis within the field of sports medicine continues to accelerate—from injury rehabilitation to injury prevention and maximizing optimum athletic performance. This trend includes not only the use of the traditional modalities such as conditioning and weight training but nutrition (supplementation), massage, and acupuncture.

Clearly the profession maintains its strong original orientation in its aggressive treatment of injured athletes. This approach has attracted those with nonsports-related problems to seek physicians and allied health personnel specializing in sports medicine; their commitment to quickly and completely restoring the individual to normal function has resulted in numerous surgical and rehabilitative treatments benefitting society in general.

Despite the growing recognition of the value of sports medicine, continuing education programs must reach out to convince managers and administrators of its value. One factor contributing to the rapid expansion and acceptance of sports medicine has been the growing number of lawsuits brought against sports organizations by players and their parents.

This situation has resulted in the joint proclamation by the American Medical Association and the National Federation of State High School Athletic Associations in the Athlete's Bill of Rights. Sports medicine personnel, coaches, and athletes should carefully examine the list.

THE ATHLETE'S BILL OF RIGHTS

Proper conditioning helps to prevent injuries by hardening the body and increasing resistance to fatigue.

1. Are the prospective players given directions and activities for preseason conditioning?
2. Is there a minimum of two weeks of practice before the game or contest?
3. Is the player required to warm up thoroughly prior to participation?
4. Are substitutions made without hesitation when players evidence disability?

Careful coaching leads to skillful performance, which lowers the incidence of injuries.

1. Is emphasis given to safety in teaching techniques and elements of play?
2. Are injuries carefully analyzed to determine causes and suggest preventative programs?
3. Are tactics discouraged that may increase the hazards and thus the incidence of injuries?
4. Are practice periods carefully planned and of reasonable duration?

Good officiating promotes the enjoyment of the game as well as the protection of players.

1. Are players as well as coaches thoroughly schooled in the rules of the games?
2. Are rules and regulations strictly enforced in practice periods as well as in games?
3. Are officials employed who are qualified both emotionally and technically for their responsibilities?

Right equipment and facilities serve a unique purpose in the protection of players.

1. Is the best protective equipment provided for contact sports?
2. Is careful attention given to proper fitting and adjustment of equipment?
3. Is equipment properly maintained, and are worn and outmoded items discarded?
4. Are proper areas for play provided and carefully maintained?

Adequate medical care is necessary in the prevention and control of athletic injuries.

1. Is there a thorough preseason health history and medical examination taken?
2. Is a physician present at contests and readily available during practice sessions?
3. Does the physician make the decision whether an athlete should return to play following injury during games?
4. Is authority from a physician required before an athlete can return to practice after being out of play because of a disabling injury?
5. Is the care given to athletes by coach or trainer limited to first aid and medically prescribed services?

The publication and dissemination of these guidelines form an important step in moving toward a safer sports environment.

THE WORLD LOVES SPORTS

The obsession with sports is a worldwide phenomenon. Each nation has added to its native sports new athletic interests. Added to the list of the U.S. exports are baseball, basketball, and football. Most recently, the World League of American Football has expanded international professional competition.

The internationalization of sports, particularly American sports, will dramatically assist the sports medicine movement as athletes and others worldwide seek to prevent and rehabilitate injuries.

WHAT IS SPORTS MEDICINE?

Unfortunately, it has become common for some health practitioners to hang out a sign proclaiming their offices to be ''sports medicine centers'' to capitalize on the public's desire for innovative and aggressive care. What really constitutes sports medicine?

As is common with developing new areas of knowledge, many definitions exist. David Lamb, past president of the American College of Sports Medicine, has stated, ''sports medicine is the scientific and medical aspects of exercise and athletics.'' Many specialties enter into achieving the objectives of sports medicine, including:

Acupuncture therapist	Health/fitness director
Athletic trainer	Massage therapist
Chiropractor	Nutritionist
Dentist	Optometrist

Exercise physiologist	Orthopedist
Orthotist	Physical therapist
Osteopath	Psychologist
Podiatrist	Strength and conditioning specialist

These individuals work as a team to achieve the goals of sports medicine. Other than athletic trainers, they all have had their education outside of sports. However, if these individuals choose their specialties early enough, they can take elective courses in sports health areas and try to obtain their clinical placement at a sports medicine center.

Professor Henry Miller, M.D., Wake Forest (North Carolina) University, divides sports medicine into three categories:

1. Athletic medicine—The evaluation, conditioning, and prevention and treatment of injuries.
2. Research—The physiological, biochemical, biomechanical, and behavioral aspects of athletic medicine; finding new methods more successful and satisfactory than the present ones.
3. Prevention and rehabilitation of chronic and degenerative disease associated with sports and athletics.

The expanded interest in sports medicine has not gone unnoticed by young people; some high schools even offer a sports medicine class as a regular elective course.

SPORTS MEDICINE COUNCIL USOC

The Sports Medicine Council of the U.S. Olympic Committee has contributed to the attention athletic health has received. The USOC Sports Medicine Program, located at the nation's Olympic Complex at Colorado Springs, Colorado, includes five areas of concentration: Clinical Services; Sports Physiology; Biomechanics; Education Services; and Special Projects. A full-time professional staff is assisted at the site by volunteer sports medicine authorities. Together they work to maximize the performance of athletes representing the United States at the Olympic and Pan American games. Thousands of fine athletes from around the nation have had the opportunity to go through the program. They have returned home healthier and more knowledgeable about sports medicine.

Kenneth (Casey) Clark, Ph.D., director of the Sports Medicine Division, believes ''the program has been a boon to the athlete—providing useful assistance when necessary to meet their goals.'' For additional information contact:

Sports Medicine Division
U.S. Olympic Committee
Olympic House
1750 East Boulder Street
Colorado Springs, CO 80909

AMERICAN COLLEGE OF SPORTS MEDICINE

Along with the fine work of the U.S. Olympic Committee Sports Medicine Division has been the contribution of the American College of Sports Medicine, which is not a college in the traditional sense but a professional society composed of over 12,000 members in 50 countries. Its constitution states that the society is

> A multidisciplinary professional and scientific society dedicated to the generation and dissemination of knowledge concerning the motivation, responses, adaptation, and health of persons engaged in exercise. Specifically, the college is concerned with:

1. Basic physiological, biochemical, biomedical and behavioral mechanisms associated with exercise.
2. Improvement and maintenance of functional capacities for daily living.
3. Prevention and rehabilitation of chronic and degenerative diseases.
4. Evaluation and conditioning of athletes.
5. Prevention and treatment of injuries related to sports and exercise.

The organization, founded in 1954, has provided guidance and knowledge to sports medicine professionals and athletes in terms of the latest athletic health procedures based upon clinic practice and serious research. The American College of Sports Medicine currently represents over 50 different professions and has five main categories of membership: member, professional in training, graduate student, undergraduate student, and associate member. An advanced membership category exists, the level of fellow, for those meeting certain criteria. The college publishes position papers and research and information publications, sponsors research grants, certifies certain sports medicine personnel, and conducts workshops and conferences. For additional information contact:

American College of Sports Medicine
401 W. Michigan Street
P.O. Box 1440
Indianapolis, IN 46206

OPPORTUNITIES IN SPORTS MEDICINE CAREERS

The work of the men and women of sports medicine is a labor of love. They seem to have very high job satisfaction, and while most have good incomes, some even have excellent salaries.

Despite the wonderfully varied backgrounds of those involved in sports medicine, they share some common threads: they have a greater interest and knowledge in science than most Americans; they have an academic orientation (most attend graduate or professional school following completion of college); they demonstrate a human-service orientation—a willingness to help people; they attempt to add new knowledge to their profession through sharing successful clinical practices and experimental research results; and they enjoy people and like athletics and sports.

Clearly one of the attractions of this field is the diversity of opportunities. Those not wishing a lengthy college commitment might consider a position as a sports physical therapy assistant, while those more academically inclined might consider the life of the sports psychologist. Similarly, within the specialties, opportunities exist for several emphases. For example, an orthopedist might have these options: working at a sports medicine center while seeing patients and conducting research or assisting a local high school as team's physician and maintaining a private practice emphasizing sports medicine.

The following chapters attempt to explain the various sports medicine careers as well as provide information about general good athletic health procedures. Not only will those considering sports medicine careers find the book of value and interest, coaches, athletes, and fans will also benefit.

CHAPTER 2

ATHLETIC TRAINING

> Training athletes is the greatest profession in the world for helping people. The athlete trainer is a 24-hour father confessor to all, both men and women, young and old. I take great pride in being an athletic trainer and a part of the N.A.T.A.
>
> Michael O'Shea, M.A., A.T.C.
> University of Louisville

In a time when many people seem to dislike their jobs, it is refreshing to find a career where the members love their duties. There are a variety of exciting career paths for athletic trainers to follow. Linda Rowan, A.T.C., serves the athletes at the University of Hawaii at Hilo. Rowan, following several injuries during her playing days at Oregon State University, became interested in sports medicine. She graduated from the university's athletic training program and received her certification. Later, she obtained an M.S. in exercise and sports science from the University of Arizona. Rowan comments, ''The hours are long and burnout can be a problem, but I love working with the local players at UHH. I enjoy this career and loved my course work, particularly those [classes] relating to the surgical implications of athletic injuries.'' UHH has served as her home for seven years.

9

At the opposite end of the nation but still among the palm trees, Andrew Clary, A.T.C., works with the players at the University of Miami in Florida. At a major university, there is a head trainer and several assistants. At Miami, Clary is the head trainer. At the much smaller Hilo, Rowan is the only trainer. Clary obtained his undergraduate degree from Purdue University and his M.A. from Florida State. At UM he not only works with many nationally famous athletes who will enter the professional ranks but also those of less stature who likewise need his skills.

Joel Safly grew up on a farm in Iowa. Presently he assists the baseball players of the Minnesota Twins affiliate, the Visalia Oaks. Safly explains, "I was always interested in sports and played everything at my small high school. This job keeps me close to the sport I love. Unfortunately, many fine young players do not know how to take care of their own body—I can help. It's nice to know that I had something to do with an athlete's success." Safly, much as a new player, paid his dues by working in baseball's rookie league. "In this league I not only served as athletic trainer but I made the players' lunches, washed the team's laundry, and drove the van to games!" He states, "It's a wonderful career because it's so rewarding."

A number of trainers serve in corporate settings, managing a fitness center for a business. Others have become entrepreneurs, owning and directing a sports medicine clinic or health club open to the public.

Athletic training serves at the core of sports medicine; of the number of careers associated with the field, only athletic training prepares its adherents directly to work in the sports field. In many ways, despite the presence of orthopedists, physical therapists, coaches, and others, trainers to a large degree determine the direction of sports medicine. And as the field expands in the future, athletic trainers will be a major part of it.

WHAT ATHLETIC TRAINERS IN SPORTS DO

Athletic trainers work within the traditions of many sports. While their duties and activities vary with the nature of their assignments, common elements exist in many athletic training positions:

1. Selecting proper equipment in cooperation with the coaching staff and the equipment manager. In this regard, new developments, such as those in podiatrics or dentistry, should be reported to the coaching staff. The athletic trainer keeps current with new developments and research findings relating to areas such as conditioning, weight training, and equipment.

2. Supervising safety factors involving playing areas. That is, the removal of items players may run into and the repair and reconditioning of equipment constituting a safety hazard.

3. Assisting in the application of injury preventive devices— such as helping and assisting with braces and similar gear and reminding athletes to utilize such equipment if necessary.

4. Planning, with the coaching staff and other sports medicine personnel, a conditioning and injury prevention program.

5. Maintaining the athletic training area and its equipment; ordering supplies, supervising the servicing of equipment, and keeping careful health records.

6. Administering first aid to injured athletes. This would involve both minor problems (for example, a sprained ankle) and major difficulties requiring transporting the player to a hospital. The trainer must also develop an emergency plan for dealing with these major difficulties.

7. Developing and supervising a rehabilitation program under the supervision of a physician and monitoring the athlete's

use of exercises. This may involve using heat, ice, sound, electricity, and mechanical devices.

8. Reporting to the coach and physician the rehabilitation progress of the athlete. This involves measuring the gain of strength in the affected area with technical equipment. This is one of the most important tasks of the trainer, as it involves determining how soon the injured player may return to action.

9. Serving as an executive and educator. As an administrator, the trainer maintains a budget, develops a student trainers program, and supervises them. Also, the trainer serves as part of the employee assistance team, which includes drug testing and insurance. In a major athletic program at a large university or with a professional team, there exists a head athletic trainer with a staff of assistant athletic trainers.

10. Establishing and maintaining good interpersonal relationships with the coaching staff, the sports medicine consultants, and the players. The trainer serves as the head of the control center: telephone calls come in on the disposition of x-rays and MRIs (magnetic resonance imaging) taken of an injured athlete, coaches call to make requests about certain safety equipment newly available, and parents call to ask about an injury their child suffered; similar other questions regularly arrive. It's not a career for someone looking for an easy job.

If it seems the athletic trainer has many tasks to perform, you are absolutely correct. The position (and the consequent duties) expand regularly. For example, the trainer now assists the equipment manager (or business manager), the coach, and the sports physician in choosing equipment. This new task is compounded by the wide variety of sports equipment now available to maximize performance—the study of shoes and sneakers alone could make a career. Some guidelines exist to assist athletic trainers in making equipment choices:

1. All equipment must meet the standards set by NOCSAE and the equipment industry.
2. Equipment must fit soundly so that it can provide maximum protection under playing conditions.
3. It must provide maximum safety for the area to be protected.
4. It must be able to withstand repeated use without a decrease in efficiency.
5. It must not impair the player's movements.
6. It must not create a hazard to other contestants. Athletic leagues and states usually have a rule against this. Normally a cast is wrapped with foam and taped by the athletic trainer if a problem exists. Usually the sports official (umpire or referee) will examine the device prior to the event as a safety check.
7. It must be replaced when no longer effective in terms of its protective value.

INJURY PREVENTION: CONDITIONING

One of the major duties of the athletic trainer involves prevention of injury not only through the utilization of equipment but by proper conditioning. Ten cardinal rules serve as guidelines for athletic trainers who wish to assist others in maximizing effectiveness (athletes can implement these principles themselves):

1. Warm Up

Athletes engage in a year-round conditioning program; however, each activity must be preceded by an adequate period of warming up. This cannot be overemphasized; a study conducted by the Duke University lacrosse coach found over 50 percent of injuries occur in the first period of a game. Many sports medicine people have observed that injuries often take place at the beginning of a practice. Consequently, it remains a must for players to warm up, even if they are late and practice has already begun. Following a warm-up period, stretching and flexibility training takes place.

2. Gradualness

Conditioning must start slowly, with the goal of peaking at a certain point in time. This will limit stiffness early in the program and hopefully eliminate staleness that may accompany over-conditioning. Setting goals at timed intervals can assist athletes in a conditioning program.

3. Timing

Athletes must receive counseling not to overdo individual work-outs or plan workouts too close together. Relaxation and rest form part of every conditioning program. Consistent overwork results in a stale competitor, increasing the likelihood of injury because of mental and physical fatigue and injury and infection due to lowered resistance. It also can result in problems with tendinitis, sprains, and more serious problems. One trend in athletic coach-ing in recent years has been the shortening of practices as the season proceeds.

4. Intensity

Practices and workouts must be characterized by quality and continuous activity (within limits) to build cardiovascular fitness. Attention must be given to heat conditioning and proper fluids for the athlete. Unfortunately some coaches permit players to stand around too much, and they cool off and may become injury victims or lose mental alertness.

5. Capacity Level

While all athletes should be cautious to avoid pitfalls, hopefully they will want to work to capacity and should be encouraged to do so. The trainer can push, if necessary, the athletes to their utmost; this means attention to nutrition and weight training to alleviate a player's deficiencies.

6. Strength

Greater endurance, stamina, speed, and confidence will result from improved strength. Weight-training equipment remains a must in this regard—not only to prevent injury but to improve athletic performance. Trainers must familiarize themselves with innovations in weight-training equipment and new concepts such as polymetrics. Naturally the training program must relate to the sport in which the athlete will engage. Most college and all professional teams will have a strength coach on a full- or part-time basis.

7. Motivation

Trainers can reinforce coaches' techniques to stimulate players. Charts in the training room showing the players' progress can prove motivational. "Nothing succeeds like success," and athletes know this better than most. Trainers can relate success stories when discussing specific conditioning strategies.

8. Specialization

Gaining knowledge about preparing for a specific athletic event enables the athletic trainer to tailor conditioning activities for a team or an athlete.

9. Relaxation

Athletic trainers should familiarize themselves with techniques of teaching players how to relax and thereby recover from tension, fatigue, and stress. Some players have experienced positive results from meditation.

10. Routine

A routine for each player carefully planned in cooperation with both the player and coach is essential. This should include daily and weekly activities. The schedule would be constructed differently depending on the time of the year—off-season, preseason, and in-season.

The athletic trainer can take much satisfaction in making a major contribution to developing a finely tuned athlete and well-conditioned team.

PROFESSIONAL ATHLETIC TEAMS

There is great diversity among the working conditions of athletic trainers; even among those who work for professional teams there exist great differences. For example, a professional indoor soccer team may utilize a trainer on a part-time basis—for practice and games. A team like this would have a contract with a sports medicine clinic to provide other medical services such as consulting and rehabilitation. A major professional team, such as a football team, may have four full-time athletic trainers. This is the case with the New York Giants professional football team.

Ronnie Barnes, M.S., A.T.C., serves as head athletic trainer for the Giants. He supervises the activities of three assistants and works with Alan Levy, M.D., the team physician, to coordinate the team's sports medicine program.

During most of the preseason (and the exhibition season) he utilizes the training facilities at Fairleigh Dickinson University at Madison, which serves as camp for the team. During the season and the off-season, he uses the fine training facilities at modern Giant's Stadium in East Rutherford, New Jersey. Barnes served as athletic trainer at East Carolina University, where he received his B.S., and at Michigan State University from which he obtained his master's degree before undertaking his present position.

Barnes, a frequent speaker at clinics and conferences, has been selected to the Eastern Carolina University Athletic Hall of Fame and several times has been named Athletic Trainer of the Year. He also has in his jewelry collection two Superbowl rings.

Serving as an athletic trainer for the New York Giants may sound glamorous, and it is—but the work load remains demanding at this level. The following schedule outlines weekly activities of the athletic training staff—assuming a Sunday game:

MONDAY

A. Supervise conditioning
B. Postgame treatments and evaluation
C. Return supplies and training room back to order after home or road game
D. Monitor weight training program
E. Complete all medical records: National Athletic Injury Reporting System

F. Report to head coach and general manager on players' health statuses (a daily task)

TUESDAY

A. Organize physicals for incoming players and those trying out for the team
B. Schedule tests, such as x-rays, for players
C. Administer treatment to reporting athletes
D. Prepare training room for weekly schedule and pay bills
E. Start to prepare travel supplies for road games
F. Make custom-fit mouth pieces and custom pads

WEDNESDAY

A. Administer treatment to reporting athletes
B. Prepractice taping
C. Medical record completion
D. Monitor team practice
E. Postpractice treatment
F. Clean training room
G. Assist orthopedist in training room

THURSDAY

A. Administer treatment to reporting athletes
B. Prepractice taping
C. Medical record completion
D. Monitor team practice
E. Postpractice treatment
F. Clean training room

FRIDAY

A. Administer treatment to reporting athletes
B. Prepractice taping
C. Medical record completion

D. Monitor team practice
E. Postpractice treatment
F. Clean training room
G. Prepare field equipment for home or away game
H. Finish packing supplies for away game

SATURDAY

A. Administer treatment to reporting athletes
B. Final preparation to all supplies for home or away game
C. Travel to away game *or*
D. Go to stadium to set up for Sunday
E. Bed check home or away games
F. Possibly stay at a hotel the night before a home game (some professional and college coaches like to stay in a motel prior to home games to hold team meetings, to remove the players from distractions, and to help the team think about the forthcoming game)

SUNDAY

A. Arrive at the stadium 3-4 hours before kickoff and prepare for the players' arrival
B. Pregame taping and last-minute pads
C. Monitor game activities
D. Postgame treatments
E. Secure supplies after each game and arrange for hospital testing if necessary

If parts of the schedule appear to be too routine, it's only the appearance—injuries, treatments, practices, and games vary.

Barnes states that he enjoys his position as one of the nation's top athletic trainers "because it permits me to work and associate with the best athletes and other health professionals who are the best at what they do." Frequently Barnes receives speaking engagement invitations and during the off-season requests to travel with other teams in other sports on short tours abroad. The off-season does not mean vacation for full-time athletic trainers with professional teams. This is a period for personal growth (reading, conferences), continued and concentrated rehabilitation of injuries following surgery, and expanded player development through weight training and conditioning.

Employment with a professional team is glamorous, exciting, and enjoyable, but it remains a difficult position to obtain, and few trainers will obtain one of these prestigious positions.

COLLEGE AND UNIVERSITY

Many opportunities exist for athletic trainers at major universities, four-year colleges, and community and junior colleges.

At the major universities involved in athletics, the working conditions will be somewhat similar to those in the professional ranks except the trainer will work with several teams during a year. The fall assignment might involve assisting the football team; in the winter, the cross country track team and basketball team; and in the spring, the baseball team and the outdoor track and field team. A major university will have a head athletic trainer, a couple of assistants, and several student trainers.

Daphne Benas, M.S., A.T.C., at Yale University, serves as head athletic trainer, administering a staff and managing a budget over $200,000. Yale has over 1,000 varsity athletes; obviously she has a demanding position.

Do not overlook career opportunities that may exist at the community (junior) college. Mike McClane, B.S., A.T.C., serves as head athletic trainer at Harper College in Illinois, a community college of 20,000 students. During the fall the college participates in the following sports: football, soccer, cross country, volleyball, golf, and tennis.

On a typical day, Mike would arrive at the training room at 11:30 A.M. From then until 2:00 he engages in evaluating previous and new injuries and providing appropriate treatment as advised by a physician. Severe cases are turned over to physicians and physical therapists. From 2:00 until 3:30 he prepares athletes for practice through taping and other support procedures. At 3:30 he leaves for the playing fields where he remains available should a problem occur. Mike sees 25 to 50 athletes a day and 3 to 8 faculty and nonathletes. At some community colleges with fewer sports, the trainer may teach a couple of courses in addition to his or her sports medicine commitment. Not all community colleges have athletic trainers, but their number continues to grow at two-year institutions.

Mike received his B.S. from De Paul University and then attended Northwestern University's School of Sports Medicine for three years of athletic training.

SCHOOLS

The role and duties vary widely among athletic trainers employed in schools. Some work at one school, such as a high school serving all sports. Others working for a school district may assist at several schools; still others teach in a school district, devoting their mornings to teaching and their afternoons to athletic training. These individuals would have certification as a teacher as well as an athletic trainer. They would receive a regular teacher's salary plus a stipend for their extra duties.

As the working conditions vary so will the facilities; most schools were not built with a training room in mind, so the trainer must utilize what he or she can. Creativity in the profession is no greater than at the school level where the trainer "makes do" with available equipment and materials. Dave Proctor, A.T.C. at Paul

G. Blazer High School in Ashland, Kentucky, cleverly utilizes worn-out automobile tires cut in half and mounted for ice baths. Pitchers on the baseball team comfortably immerse the elbow area after pitching. Trainers must learn to improvise to achieve their purposes.

The employment potential at the school level will surely expand during the 1990s. Most school districts now employ an athletic trainer part time or full time. North Carolina became the first state to require every high school to have an athletic trainer beginning in 1985. Many other states have similar laws under consideration; hopefully by the end of the decade they will be in place.

SPORTS MEDICINE CLINIC OR CENTER

The growth of interest in sports medicine has been accompanied by the development of sports medicine clinics or centers. These organizations work with individual athletes and sports teams. Some are associated with colleges, such as the Temple University Center for Sports Medicine and Science (Pennsylvania); others are privately owned and operated, such as the Sports Fitness Institute in Glen Ellyn, Illinois. Hospital affiliation exists as another form; for example, the Mercy-Haverford Community Hospital Wellness Center.

Many athletic trainers work at a wide variety of facilities, including corporate, university, private, and hospital related.

One interesting program is the Alfred I. DuPont Institute's Injury Prevention Program in Delaware. The program, a service of the institute's Division of Sports Medicine, seeks to provide "a medically supervised training routine for adolescents from 12 to 20 years of age." The students receive an assessment of their health at the beginning of the program and then "a training regimen geared to their sport." Under Karen Ave, sports medicine coordinator, young people have access to a wide variety of sports medicine professionals and equipment to assist them in meeting their goals.

EDUCATION

Individuals in high school wishing to enter this field should begin as soon as possible to develop an interest and expertise in science. Students should attend a CPR program for certification and a First Aid course if these programs are available. At the college level, course work is focused on the sciences.

Montclair State College

Many undergraduate programs exist that lead to certification in athletic training. Typical is Montclair State College in New Jersey. Students take a range of liberal arts, science, physical education, and other courses. Some of those taken in the specialty area include Basic Prevention and Care of Athletic Injuries, Advanced Prevention and Care of Athletic Injuries, and Internship in Athletic Training. The last course, common to all NATA (National Athletic Trainers Association)-approved programs, requires the student to spend several hundred hours working with a certified trainer.

THE UNITED STATES SPORTS ACADEMY

A number of programs exist at the graduate level to service people who wish to change careers or further their professional growth. One unique program is at the U.S. Sports Academy in Mobile, Alabama. The academy, founded in 1972, functions as a postgraduate institute granting only the master's degree. In the area of sports medicine the following are sample courses:

- *Sport Medicine I:* Anatomy and kinesiology, related to recognition and evaluation of athletic injuries, proper preventive and first aid procedures for athletic injuries.
- *Sport Medicine II:* Nervous system related to human movement; nutrition as related to physical activity; evaluation procedures for athletic injuries; advanced taping and protective devices; pharmacology related to athletics; and legal aspects of care and prevention of injuries.

Similar courses and electives round out the students' program.

The Adelphi University Program

Typical of the many new and expanding programs in sports medicine is the program at Adelphi University in Garden City, New York. Operating under the chairpersonship of Ron Feingold, Ph.D., the Department of Physical Education changed its name and direction. While retaining the traditional programs in physical education, the department expanded to newer areas—exercise physiology, athletic training, sports management, and sports medicine. The department's new name, the Department of Physical and Human Performance Science, reflects its recent innovations.

At the undergraduate level, the students' program includes university requirements, departmental requirements, and electives. Students in the athletic training program fulfill several requirements; the following are examples:

Scientific Foundations of Physical Activity
Sports Medicine
Kinesiology
Exercise Physiology
First Aid and Injury Control

Conditioning/Fitness Program

Additional courses are taken in consultation with an adviser to complete the student's program. These include a wide variety of sports courses—ice skating, squash, beginning golf, lifeguarding, sailing, horseback riding, weight training, and others. Many opportunities exist to grow personally and professionally through the electives. The course description for two sample courses follows.

- *First Aid and Injury Control:* Prevention and treatment of injuries in athletic and physical education activities, including first aid procedures, massage, preventive and protective taping, and therapeutic exercises. Lab experience. First aid and CPR certification.
- *Kinesiology:* An analysis of the skeletal, muscular, and nervous system provides the basis for understanding human movements and, in particular, movement in various sports skills and dance forms. Mechanical principles underlying movement and their relationship to the performance of skills.

Dr. Feingold places the emphasis in the sports medicine program on wellness, injury prevention, and interdisciplinary approaches to problems; this philosophy is reflected in all the courses. At the graduate level, Adelphi University offers a master's degree in exercise physiology with special emphasis in a variety of areas as well as more traditional programs such as physical education, special physical education, and sports management. The exercise physiology specialization has emphasis areas in adult fitness/cardiac rehabilitation, sports medicine, aging, or research. At this level the curriculum reflects more advanced content. For example, biomechanics (a course that requires students to have a background in kinesiology or scientific foundations of physical activity) carries the following description: "Body framework and architecture, and neuromuscular considerations as applied to human movement. Analysis of movement and its application to teaching and coaching of motor skills.''

At Adelphi University, Dr. Feingold has recognized a noticeable movement of allied health personnel and special physical education instructors into the graduate sports medicine program. This, he believes, is the result of the ''greater satisfaction that can be obtained in working with healthy individuals who work 1,000 percent to regain utilization of the injured part.'' He feels that too often the average person does not try hard enough to return from an injury, and when therapists or nurses try encouragement, they are often resisted by the patient.

''The job market is unlimited now and in the future,'' states Dr. Feingold, speaking of career opportunities in sports medicine. The public realizes the value of fitness and nutrition and expects appropriate use of sports medicine for local teams, for professional teams, and for individuals. Feingold further mentions that ''women's opportunities are excellent in athletic training—many schools are looking to add athletic medicine specialists to work with their female athletes.''

Feingold recommends that high school students take the following courses: mathematics and sciences—biology, chemistry, and physics. The sciences are a must, and mathematics will help with college science courses; psychology and sociology—because those in the sports medicine field must be people oriented; computers—in the future computers will assist in planning, conditioning, and rehabilitation programs.

THE FUTURE

One of the careers of the future will be that of athletic trainer. Participants in this field love the challenges, and the career opportunities are growing. While salaries remain only moderate to good (at the low end of the scale for a professional, approximately $30,000–$100,000 a year), potential salaries will expand in the years ahead. ''The athletic trainer has come a long way since the water bucket and sponge,'' states trainer Mike O'Shea. As with all professional organizations, certification today is a must. The major organization, the National Athletic Trainers Association, certifies trainers and evaluates college athletic training programs. For additional information, contact:

National Athletic Trainers Association
2952 Stemmons Freeway
Suite 200
Dallas, TX 75247-6103

You may also wish to examine the fine NATA journal, *Athletic Training;* it contains a variety of articles by sports medicine personnel as well as professional information. Another book worth reading, *Modern Athletic Training,* may be obtained from Cramer Educational Services, P.O. Box 1001, Gardner, Kansas 66030.

NATIONAL ATHLETIC TRAINERS ASSOCIATION APPROVED ATHLETIC TRAINING EDUCATION PROGRAMS

The colleges listed below offer programs for the education of athletic trainers; some schools offer undergraduate curriculum, others graduate; some offer course work at both levels.

Alabama

Director, Athletic Training Program
Samford University
Department of Health, PE, and Recreation
Birmingham, AL 35229

Arizona

Director, Athletic Training Program
Department of Exercise and Sport Science
University of Arizona
Tucson, AZ 85721

California

Director, Athletic Training Program
Department of Physical Education and Recreation
California State University, Fresno
Fresno, CA 93740

Director, Athletic Training Program
Department of Health, Physical Education and Recreation
California State University, Fullerton
Fullerton, CA 92634

Director, Athletic Training Program
Department of Physical Education
California State University, Long Beach
Long Beach, CA 90840

Director, Athletic Training Program
Department of Physical Education and Athletics
California State University, Northridge
Northridge, CA 91324

Director, Athletic Training Program
Department of Athletics and Sport
California State University, Sacramento
Sacramento, CA 95819

Director, Athletic Training Program
Department of Human Performance
California State University, San Jose
San Jose, CA 95192

Delaware

Director, Athletic Training Program
Department of Physical Education, Athletics and Recreation
University of Delaware
Newark, DE 19711

Florida

Director, Athletic Training Program
Department of Exercise and Sport Science
Gainesville, FL 32604

Idaho

Director, Athletic Training Program
Department of Physical Education
Boise State University
Boise, ID 83725

Illinois

Director, Athletic Training Program
Department of Physical Education
Southern Illinois University
Carbondale, IL 62901

Director, Athletic Training Program
School of Health, Physical Education and Recreation
Eastern Illinois University
Charleston, IL 61920

Director, Athletic Training Program
College of Health, Physical Education and Recreation
Western Illinois University
Macomb, IL 61455

Director, Athletic Training Program
Department of Health, Physical Education and Dance
Illinois State University
Normal, IL 61761

Director, Athletic Training Program
Department of Physical Education or Department of Kinesiology
University of Illinois
Urbana, IL 61801

Indiana

Director, Athletic Training Program
Athletic Department
Anderson University
Anderson, IN 46012

Director, Athletic Training Program
School of Health, Physical Education and Recreation
Indiana University
Bloomington, IN 47401

Director, Athletic Training Program
Department of Men's Physical Education
Ball State University
Muncie, IN 47306

Director, Athletic Training Program
School of Health, Physical Education and Recreation
Indiana State University
Terre Haute, IN 47809

Director, Athletic Training Program
Department of Physical Education, Health and Recreation Studies
Purdue University
West Lafayette, IN 47907

Iowa

Director, Athletic Training Program
Department of Exercise Science and Physical Education
University of Iowa
Iowa City, IA 52242

Kansas

Director, Athletic Training Program
Department of Physical Education, Dance and Leisure Studies
Kansas State University
Manhattan, KS 66506

Kentucky

Director, Athletic Training Program
College of Health, Physical Education, Recreation and Athletics
Eastern Kentucky University
Richmond, KY 40475

Massachusetts

Director, Athletic Training Program
Department of Physical Education
Northeastern University
Boston, MA 02115

Director, Athletic Training Program
Department of Physical Education
Bridgewater State College
Bridgewater, MA 02324

Director, Athletic Training Program
Division of Health, Physical Education and Recreation
Springfield College
Springfield, MA 01109

Michigan

Director, Athletic Training Program
Department of Physical Education and Athletics
Grand Valley State College
Allendale, MI 49401

Director, Athletic Training Program
Department of Health, Physical Education and Recreation
Western Michigan University
Kalamazoo, MI 49009

Director, Athletic Training Program
Physical Education Department
Central Michigan University
Mount Pleasant, MI 48859

Minnesota

Director, Athletic Training Program
Physical Education Department
Mankato State University
Mankato, MN 56001

Director, Athletic Training Program
Department of Health, Physical Education and Athletics
Gustavus Adolphus College
St. Paul, MN 56082

Mississippi

Director, Athletic Training Program
Department of Athletic Administration and Coaching
University of Southern Mississippi
Hattiesburg, MS 39401

Missouri

Director, Athletic Training Program
Department of Physical Education
Southwest Missouri State University
901 S. National
Springfield, MO 65802

Montana

Director, Athletic Training Program
Department of Health and Physical Education
University of Montana
Missoula, MT 59801

Nebraska

Director, Athletic Training Program
Department of Health, Physical Education and Recreation
University of Nebraska
Lincoln, NE 68588

Nevada

Director, Athletic Training Program
Department of Health, Physical Education, Recreation and Dance
University of Nevada–Las Vegas
Las Vegas, NV 89119

New Jersey

Director, Athletic Training Program
Department of Physical Education
Kean College of New Jersey
Union, NJ 07083

Director, Athletic Training Program
Department of Movement Sciences and Leisure Studies
William Patterson College of New Jersey
Wayne, NJ 07470

New Mexico

Director, Athletic Training Program
Department of Health, Physical Education and Recreation
University of New Mexico
Albuquerque, NM 87131

Director, Athletic Training Program
Department of Physical Education, Recreation and Dance
New Mexico State University
Las Cruces, NM 88003

New York

Director, Athletic Training Program
Department of Physical Education
Canisius College
Buffalo, NY 14208

Director, Athletic Training Program
Division of Health, Physical Education and Recreation
SUNY–Cortland
Cortland, NY 13045

Director, Athletic Training Program
Department of Physical Education and Exercise Science
SUNY–Buffalo
Buffalo, NY 14214

Director, Athletic Training Program
Department of Health, Physical Education and Recreation
Ithaca College
Ithaca, NY 14850

North Carolina

Director, Athletic Training Program
Department of Health, Physical Education and Recreation
Appalachian State University
Boone, NC 28608

Director, Athletic Training Program
Department of Physical Education
University of North Carolina
Chapel Hill, NC 27514

Director, Athletic Training Program
Department of Health, Physical Education, Recreation and Safety
East Carolina University
Greenville, NC 27834

North Dakota

Director, Athletic Training Program
Department of Health, Physical Education, Recreation and Athletics
North Dakota State University
Fargo, ND 58102

Director, Athletic Training Program
Department of Health, Physical Education and Recreation
University of North Dakota
Grand Forks, ND 58201

Ohio

Director, Athletic Training Program
Department of Physical Education, Health, Sports Management and
    Intercollegiate Athletics
Mount Union College
Alliance, OH 45701

Director, Athletic Training Program
School of Health, Physical Education and Recreation
Ohio University
Athens, OH 45701

Director, Athletic Training Program
School of Health, Physical Education and Recreation
Bowling Green State University
Bowling Green, OH 43403

Director, Athletic Training Program
Department of Sports Medicine
Marietta College
Marietta, OH 45750

Director, Athletic Training Program
Withrow Court, Room 6
Miami University of Ohio
Oxford, OH 45056

Director, Athletic Training Program
Department of Physical Education
Toledo University
Toledo, OH 43606

Oregon

Director, Athletic Training Program
Physical Education Department
Oregon State University
Corvallis, OR 97331

Director, Athletic Training Program
Department of Physical Education
University of Oregon
Eugene, OR 97403

Pennsylvania

Director, Athletic Training Program
College of Education
California University of Pennsylvania
California, PA 15419

Director, Athletic Training Program
Koehler Fieldhouse
East Stroudsburg University
East Stroudsburg, PA 18301

Director, Athletic Training Program
School of Health, Physical Education and Recreation
Lock Haven University
Lock Haven, PA 17745

Director, Athletic Training Program
Department of Physical Education
Temple University
Philadelphia, PA 19122

Director, Athletic Training Program
Health, Physical Education and Recreation
University of Pittsburgh
Pittsburgh, PA 15261

Director, Athletic Training Program
Health Sciences Department
Slippery Rock State College
Slippery Rock, PA 16057

Director, Athletic Training Program
College of Health, Physical Education and Recreation
Pennsylvania State University
University Park, PA 16802

Director, Athletic Training Program
Physical Education Department
West Chester State College
West Chester, PA 19380

South Dakota

Director, Athletic Training Program
Department of Health, Physical Education and Recreation
South Dakota State University
Brookings, SD 57007

Tennessee

Director, Athletic Training Program
Department of Physical Education and Recreation
East Tennessee State University
Johnson City, TN 35614

Texas

Director, Athletic Training Program
Department of Athletics
Texas Christian University
Fort Worth, TX 76129

Director, Athletic Training Program
Department of Health and Physical Education
Southwest Texas State University
San Marcos, TX 78666

Utah

Director, Athletic Training Program
Department of Physical Education and Sports
Brigham Young University
Provo, UT 84602

Vermont

Director, Athletic Training Program
Department of Human Development Studies
University of Vermont
Burlington, VT 05405

Virginia

Director, Athletic Training Program
Department of Health and Physical Education
University of Virginia
Charlottesville, VA 22903

Director, Athletic Training Program
Department of Health and Physical Education
James Madison University
Harrisonburg, VA 22807

Director, Athletic Training Program
Department of Intercollegiate Athletics
Old Dominion University
Norfolk, VA 23508

Washington

Director, Athletic Training Program
Department of Physical Education for Men and Women
Washington State University
Pullman, WA 99163

West Virginia

Director, Athletic Training Program
Department of Health, Physical Education and Recreation
Marshall University
Huntington, WV 25701

Director, Athletic Training Program
Department of Professional Physical Education
West Virginia University
Morgantown, WV 26505

Wisconsin

Director, Athletic Training Program
150 Mitchell Hall
University of Wisconsin–La Crosse
La Crosse, WI 54601

CHAPTER 3

SPORTS PHYSICAL THERAPISTS

Physical therapy is an art and a science which contributes to the promotion of health and prevention of disease through understanding of body movement. It functions in the prevention, correction, and alleviation of the effects of disease and injury. Methods include evaluation and treatment of patients, administration, and supervision of physical therapy services and personnel, consultation with other health disciplines, preparation of records and reports, participation in community planning and projects, and implementation and accreditation of educational programs.

Professor Thelma Holmes
University of Florida

DUTIES AND ACTIVITIES

Obviously most physical therapists do not work with athletes but with the general public. Those involved in sports normally work at sports medicine clinics or centers, have their own private office practice in which they emphasize working with athletes, or serve as consultants to teams and schools. Many sports medicine centers employ orthopedists, athletic trainers, and physical therapists. These sports medicine personnel function as a team, with the therapist emphasizing the rehabilitation aspects of the clinic's goals.

Some sports physical therapists (PTs) start their own clinics. Cindy Tumas, M.A., R.P.T., presently owns and directs the Southern Delaware Physical Therapy and Sports Institute (Dover, Delaware). She and her staff assist high school and college athletes as well as the general public. Cindy received her undergraduate education at Ithaca College (New York) and her master's degree in physical therapy from Stanford University (California). Following work at a number of sports medicine centers, including the world-famous Kerlan-Jobe Orthopedic Clinic (serving professional athletes and others) in Los Angeles, Tumas opened the institute in 1988; undoubtedly its success is a result of her sports medicine team and her entrepreneurial spirit. Many physical therapists are moving into opening such centers; if you think this is in your future, take business courses as your electives in college.

Physical therapists have a number of techniques at their disposal to aid the athlete in returning to competition, including:

- *Hydrotherapy*—The use of heated water in a whirlpool. The water moves by a jet of air. This method increases circulation and relaxes the muscles.
- *Contrast baths*—Often used in conjunction with the whirlpool. The patient alternates the affected part between warm and cold water at timed intervals. Athletes with sprained ankles often receive this therapy.
- *Paraffin baths*—A mixture of paraffin (a wax) and mineral oil heated to a hot temperature. Sometimes this technique is used to aid athletes with elbow problems.
- *Hot packs*—Square pads containing a mixture of silicon, gelatin, and chemicals to retain heat. Historically these have been used to reduce back and neck pain among athletes.

- *Diathermy*—A heating technique that goes deep to produce relief to muscle tissues and joints.
- *Ultrasound*—Serves a similar function as diathermy; however, this method uses ultrasound waves for short periods of time.
- *Massage*—A number of innovative types of massage have appeared on the scene. This technique, properly used in conjunction with other healing strategies, can aid the injured player.

Readers are strongly urged not to apply any of the above strategies on themselves following an injury; it's possible through improper treatment to do more damage than good. A physical therapist should coordinate all recoveries.

Physical therapists have continued to add procedures and equipment to their ''bag of tricks.'' In recent years many therapists have moved from heat to cold therapy for rehabilitation. While some traditional devices such as traction remain, innovations such as acutherapy (acupuncture; acupressure) move the profession forward. Very recently success has come from the use of electrical current to relieve pain and to promote the healing of bones.

In addition to healing skills, physical therapists must have good interpersonal abilities. They not only need to work with patients but a wide range of health care personnel from radiologists and radiologic technicians to orthopedists and orthotists. A college education is a must.

EDUCATION

There are many colleges for the aspiring therapist to attend. Typical of these programs is the one at Ball State University in Muncie, Indiana. Students take courses such as the following:

Introduction to Physical Therapy
Medical Sciences—Pathology, Pharmacology
Patient Evaluation and Treatment by Nerve and
    Muscle Stimulating Currents

The following description of courses explain the learning activities covered in some of the program's courses:

- *Physical Agents:* Lectures, laboratory practice, and clinical practice in massage, traction, and conductive heat and cold.
- *Advanced Therapeutic Exercise:* Lecture and laboratory practice in the neurological bases for therapeutic exercise, including normal and abnormal growth and development.

The University of Central Arkansas in Conway offers a variety of programs in physical therapy: a two-year program that qualifies the candidate for PT assistant; and a bachelor's (B.S.)- and master's-level (M.S.) degree program that leads to qualifying the student for PT examinations. The completion of the program and successful state board testing results in the title registered physical therapist, or R.P.T.

The student in the graduate program at CAU takes courses such as Sports Physical Therapy: The Upper Extremities—presents a regional perspective of upper extremity function as it relates to athletes; Foundations of Sports Physical Therapy—provides basic knowledge and skill required to successfully treat the injured athlete and develop and implement a sports physical therapy program; Cardiopulmonary Physical Therapy—an in-depth exploration of pathophysiology related to cardiovascular and respiratory systems.

Students in most colleges also pursue a regular complement of required courses. In addition to their professional area courses and electives, they may wish to take work in sports studies and sciences, such as in athletic training.

Following graduation, students must be licensed by the state in which they wish to practice. All 50 states, the Commonwealth of Puerto Rico, and the District of Columbia require such professional licensing; 49 of the states require passing of an examination prepared by the state board of medical examiners.

Many therapists pursue graduate studies to keep pace with the rapid developments in their profession. In addition, they wish to qualify themselves for leadership positions in their workplace and in the educational and service organizations to which physical therapists belong. Many colleges offer such programs.

The close contact between the therapist and the injured athlete has resulted in the recent development of a code of ethics for the profession. Designed to provide guidelines by which therapists may determine their conduct, the code follows:

CODE OF ETHICS

PREAMBLE

This Code of Ethics sets forth ethical principles for the physical therapy profession. Members of this profession are responsible for maintaining and promoting ethical practice. This Code of Ethics adopted by the American Physical Therapy Association, shall be binding on the physical therapists who are members of the Association.

PRINCIPLE 1

Physical therapists respect the rights and dignity of all individuals.

PRINCIPLE 2

Physical therapists comply with the laws and regulations governing the practice of physical therapy.

PRINCIPLE 3

Physical therapists accept responsibility for the exercise of sound judgement.

PRINCIPLE 4

Physical therapists maintain and promote high standards in the provision of physical therapy services.

PRINCIPLE 5

Physical therapists seek remuneration for their services that is deserved and reasonable.

PRINCIPLE 6

Physical therapists provide accurate information to the consumer about the profession and about those services they provide.

PRINCIPLE 7

Physical therapists accept the responsibility to protect the public and the profession from unethical, incompetent or illegal acts.

Phenomenal advances in surgery have resulted in major changes in postoperative care and rehabilitation. For example, today, through the miracle of arthroscopic procedures, a rehabilitation program can begin the same day as the surgery. The impact on athletes and those physical therapists who work with them is obvious.

The attraction of the general field of physical therapy grows daily as surveys continue to label it a profession of improving job opportunities (one of the best) and a career with significantly growing salaries. Within the field exist sports physical therapists who will even exceed their fellow PTs in job opportunities and salary. Recently the national professional organization, APTA (America Physical Therapy Association), designated a specialty section for sports physical therapists which requires advanced study and board certification. These individuals will serve in the forefront of their profession during the decades ahead. For example, historically, PTs have worked with injured or recovering athletes. Now, as their role expands as a member of the sports medicine team, they have a serious concern for the prevention of injury. As with all sports medicine careers, the job of the sport PT will continue to evolve.

Clearly this profession offers opportunity for maximum job satisfaction and for a fine standard of living for its membership. For additional information, read *Opportunities in Physical Therapy Careers* from the VGM Career Horizons series; the following books are available from the American Physical Therapy Association (see address below):

Anatomy the Trunk: A Review
Functional Anatomy of the Shoulder Complex: A Review
The Hip Joint
The Knee: Athletic Injuries
Neural Regulation of Cardiovascular Response to Exercise
Physical Therapy Practice in Educational Environments: Policies, Guidelines, and Background Information—An Anthology
The Problem-Oriented Approach to Physical Therapy Care
Stress: How to Recognize It—What to Do about It Research—Anthology

In addition, you may wish to examine the association's magazine, *Physical Therapy* (available from the address below). It contains articles on rehabilitation, information on the profession, and advertisements on the equipment available to the therapist. For the above materials and additional information, contact:

American Physical Therapy Association
1111 North Fairfax Street
Alexandria, VA 22314

Another periodical with valuable information for those considering the PT field is *Rehab Management*; it contains articles such as "Sports Injury Management" and "Taking a Proactive Approach to Sports Medicine Injuries." It may be purchased from:

Rehab Management
1849 Sawtelle Boulevard, Suite 770
Los Angeles, CA 90025

AMERICAN PHYSICAL THERAPY ASSOCIATION ACCREDITED ENTRY-LEVEL PROFESSIONAL PROGRAMS FOR PHYSICAL THERAPISTS

The American Physical Therapy Association is recognized as an accrediting agency for programs in physical therapy in the U.S. Department of Education and the Council on Postsecondary Accreditation. Accreditation is the ongoing process by which an agency evaluates a program of study as meeting certain predetermined standards and criteria. The following educational programs are recognized as accredited professional programs for physical therapists.

Alabama

University of Alabama in Birmingham
Division of Physical Therapy
RTI Building., Room 004
Birmingham, AL 35294

University of South Alabama
Department of Physical Therapy, Division of Allied Health
    Professions
2000 Brookley Center, Room 210
Mobile, AL 36688

Arizona

Northern Arizona University
Department of Physical Therapy, School of Health Professions
C.U. Box 15105
Flagstaff, AZ 86011

Arkansas

University of Central Arkansas
Department of Physical Therapy
Conway, AR 72032

California

California State University at Fresno
Physical Therapy Program
School of Health and Social Work
Fresno, CA 93740

Loma Linda University
Department of Physical Therapy, School of Allied Health
    Professions
Loma Linda, CA 92350

California State University at Long Beach
Physical Therapy Department, School of Allied Arts Sciences
1250 Bellflower Boulevard
Long Beach, CA 90840

Children's Hospital of Los Angeles/Chapman College
School of Physical Therapy
4650 Sunset Boulevard
Los Angeles, CA 90027

Mount Saint Mary's College
Programs in Physical Therapy
12001 Chalon Road
Los Angeles, CA 90049

University of Southern California
Department of Physical Therapy
2025 Zonal Avenue, CSA-208
Los Angeles, CA 90033

California State University at Northridge
Curriculum in Physical Therapy, Health Science Department
Northridge, CA 91330

University of California
Curriculum in Physical Therapy, School of Medicine
Box 0736
San Francisco, CA 94143

University of the Pacific
Physical Therapy Department
Stockton, CA 95211

Colorado

University of Colorado
Curriculum in Physical Therapy
Health Science Center
4200 E. Ninth Avenue
Box C244
Denver, CO 80262

Connecticut

Quinnipiac College
School of Allied Health and Natural Sciences, Physical Therapy
   Program
515 Sherman Avenue
Hamden, CT 06518

University of Connecticut
School of Allied Health Professions, Program in Physical Therapy
U 101
Storrs, CT 06269-2101

Delaware

University of Delaware
Physical Therapy Program, School of Life and Health Sciences
054 McKinly Lab
Newark, DE 19716

District of Columbia

Howard University
Department of Physical Therapy, College of Allied Health
    Sciences
Annex I, Room B-29
6th and Bryant Streets
Washington, DC, NW 20059

Florida

University of Miami
Programs in Physical Therapy, Department of Orthopedics and
    Rehabilitation
5915 Ponce de Leon Boulevard, 5th Floor
Coral Gables, FL 33146

University of Florida
Department of Physical Therapy–College of Health Related
    Professions
POB J-154, JHMHC
Gainesville, FL 32610

Florida International University
Department of Physical Therapy, College of Health Sciences
Tamiami Trail
Miami, FL 33199

Florida A.&M. University
Division of Physical Therapy
Tallahassee, FL 32307

Georgia

Emory University
Division of Physical Therapy
1441 Clifton Road SE
Atlanta, GA 30322

Georgia State University
Department of Physical Therapy, School of Allied Health
    Sciences
University Plaza
Atlanta, GA 30303

Medical College of Georgia
Department of Physical Therapy, School of Allied Health
    Sciences
Augusta, GA 30912-3100

Illinois

Northwestern University
Programs in Physical Therapy, Medical School
345 E. Superior Street, Room 1323
Chicago, IL 60611

University of Health Sciences, Chicago Medical School
Physical Therapy Program, School of Related Health Sciences
3333 N. Green Bay Road
Chicago, IL 60064

University of Illinois (Medical Center) at Chicago
Department of Physical Therapy, College of Associated Health
    Professions
1919 W. Taylor Street
Chicago, IL 60612

Northern Illinois University
Physical Therapy Program, School of Allied Health Professions
217 Williston
DeKalb, IL 60115

Indiana

University of Evansville
Department of Physical Therapy
1800 Lincoln Avenue
Evansville, IN 47722

Indiana University
Physical Therapy Program, Division of Allied Health Sciences
School of Medicine
1140 W. Michigan Street, CF 326
Indianapolis, IN 46223

University of Indianapolis
Krannert Graduate School of Physical Therapy
1400 E. Hanna Avenue
Indianapolis, IN 46227-3697

Iowa

University of Osteopathic Medicine and Health Sciences
Physical Therapy Program
College of Biological Sciences
3200 Grand Avenue
Des Moines, IA 50312

University of Iowa
Physical Therapy Education Program
2600 Steindler Building
Iowa City, IA 52242

Kansas

University of Kansas Medical Center
Department of Physical Therapy
1002 Hinch Hall
Kansas City, KS 66103

Wichita State University
Department of Physical Therapy, College of Health Related
    Professions
Box 43
Wichita, KS 67208-1595

Kentucky

University of Kentucky Medical Center
Department of Physical Therapy
Room 4, Annex 1
Lexington, KY 40536-0079

University of Louisville
Physical Therapy Program
Carmichael Building
525 E. Madison Street
Louisville, KY 40292

Louisiana

Louisiana State University Medical Center
Department of Physical Therapy, Allied Health Professions Annex
P.O. Box 33932
Shreveport, LA 71130-3932

Maine

University of New England
Department of Physical Therapy
11 Hills Beach Road
Biddeford, ME 04005

Maryland

University of Maryland
Department of Physical Therapy, School of Medicine
32 S. Greene Street
Baltimore, MD 21201

University of Maryland Eastern Shore
Department of Physical Therapy
P.O. Box 1061
Princess Anne, MD 21853

Massachusetts

Boston University
Department of Physical Therapy
Sargeant College of Allied Health Professions
635 Commonwealth Avenue
Boston, MA 02115

Northeastern University
Department of Physical Therapy
6 Robinson Hall
360 Huntington Avenue
Boston, MA 02115

Simmons College
Graduate Program in Physical Therapy
300 The Senway
Boston, MA 02115

University of Lowell
Program in Physical Therapy
200 Weed Hall–South Campus
Lowell, MA 01854

Springfield College
Department of Physical Therapy
263 Alden Street
Springfield, MA 01109

Michigan

Grand Valley State University
Physical Therapy Program–School of Health Sciences
Allendale, MI 49401

Andrews University
Department of Physical Therapy
Berrien Springs, MI 49104

Wayne State University
Department of Physical Therapy
College of Pharmacy and Allied Health Professions
439 Health Sciences Building
Detroit, MI 48202

University of Michigan
Physical Therapy Department
Flint, MI 48502-2186

Oakland University
Program in Physical Therapy
School of Health Sciences
Rochester, MI 48309-4401

Minnesota

College of St. Scholastica
Department of Physical Therapy
1200 Kenwood Avenue
Duluth, MN 55811

University of Minnesota
Program in Physical Therapy
Box 388, UMHC
Minneapolis, MN 55455

Mayo Foundation
Physical Therapy Program, School of Health Related Sciences
1104 Siebens Building
Rochester, MN 55905

Mississippi

University of Mississippi Medical Center
Department of Physical Therapy
2500 N. State Street
Jackson, MS 39216

Missouri

University of Missouri
Physical Therapy Program, School of Health Related Professions
120 Lewis Hall
Columbia, MO 65211

Rockhurst College
Physical Therapy Program
5225 Troost Avenue
Kansas City, MO 64110

Maryville College
Department of Physical Therapy
13550 Conway Road
St. Louis, MO 63141

University of Missouri Medical Center
Physical Therapy Department
1504 S. Grand Boulevard, Room 306
St. Louis, MO 63104

Washington University
Program in Physical Therapy, School of Medicine
660 S. Euclid Avenue, Box 8083
St. Louis, MO 63110

Montana

University of Montana
Physical Therapy Program
Missoula, MT 59812

Nebraska

University of Nebraska Medical Center
Division of Physical Therapy Education, College of Medicine
600 S. 42d
Omaha, NE 68198-4420

New Jersey

Rutgers, The State University of New Jersey
Graduate School–Camden University of Medicine and Dentistry
    of New Jersey
School of Health Related Professions
401 Haddon Avenue
Camden, NJ 08103-1506

Kean College of New Jersey/University of Medicine and Dentistry
    of New Jersey
Physical Therapy Program, School of Allied Health Professions
65 Bergen Street
Newark, NJ 07103-3007

Stockton State College
Physical Therapy Program
Jim Lees Road
Pomana, NJ 08240

New Mexico

University of New Mexico
Division of Physical Therapy
Allied Health Sciences Center
Albuquerque, NM 87131

New York

Daemen College
Physical Therapy Curriculum
4380 Main Street
Amherst, NY 14226

Long Island University
Division of Physical Therapy
University Plaza
Brooklyn, NY 11201

State University of New York, Health Science Center at Brooklyn
Physical Therapy Program
Box 16, 450 Clarkson Avenue
Brooklyn, NY 11203

State University of New York at Buffalo
Physical Therapy Program
416 Kimball Tower–Main Street Campus
Buffalo, NY 14214

Touro College
Physical Therapy Program
Building 10
135 Carmen Road
Dix Hills, NY 11746

Ithaca College
Division of Physical Therapy
Ithaca, NY 14850

Columbia University
Program in Physical Therapy
630 W. 168th Street
New York, NY 10032

Hunter College
Physical Therapy Program, School of Health Sciences
425 E. 25th Street
New York, NY 10010

New York University
Department of Physical Therapy
Basic Science Building
433 First Avenue
New York, NY 10010

State University of New York at Stony Brook
Department of Physical Therapy, School of Allied Health
        Professions
Health Sciences Center
Stony Brook, NY 11794

State University of New York Health Science Center at Syracuse
Physical Therapy Program, College of Health Related Professions
750 E. Adams Street
Syracuse, NY 13210

Russell Sage College
Department of Physical Therapy
Troy, NY 12180

North Carolina

University of North Carolina
Division of Physical Therapy, Department of Medical Allied
    Health Professions
Medical School Wing E222H-CB#7135
Chapel Hill, NC 72599-7135

Duke University
Medical Center, Department of Physical Therapy
POB# 3965
Durham, NC 27710

East Carolina University
Department of Physical Therapy, School of Allied Health and
    Social Professions
Greenville, NC 27858-4353

North Dakota

University of North Dakota
Department of Physical Therapy, School of Medicine
Grand Forks, ND 58201

Ohio

Ohio University
School of Physical Therapy
Room 199, Convocation Center
Athens, OH 45701

Cleveland State University
Physical Therapy Department
Department of Health Sciences
1983 E. 24th Street, Fenn Tower 609
Cleveland, OH 44115

Ohio State University
Division of Physical Therapy, School of Allied Medical
    Professions
1583 Perry Street
Columbus, OH 43210

Medical College of Ohio
Physical Therapy Program, School of Allied Health
P.O. Box 10008
Toledo, OH 43699-0008

Oklahoma

Langston University
Physical Therapy Program
Langston, OK 73050

University of Oklahoma
Department of Physical Therapy
Health Sciences Center
POB 26901
Oklahoma City, OK 73190

Oregon

Pacific University
Department of Physical Therapy
2043 College Way
Forest Grove, OR 97116

Pennsylvania

Beaver College
Department of Physical Therapy
Glenside, PA 19038

Hahnemann University
Physical Therapy Program
201 N. 15th Street
Philadelphia, PA 19102

Philadelphia College of Pharmacy and Science
Physical Therapy Department
43d Street and Woodland Avenue
Philadelphia, PA 19107

Temple University
Department of Physical Therapy, College of Allied Health
    Professions
3307 North Broad Street
Philadelphia, PA 19140

Thomas Jefferson University
Department of Physical Therapy–College of Allied Health
    Sciences
103 South 9th Street
Philadelphia, PA 19107

University of Pittsburgh
Department of Physical Therapy
101 Pennsylvania
Pittsburgh, PA 15261

Puerto Rico

University of Puerto Rico
College of Health Related Professions
Medical Science Campus
GPO Box 5067
San Juan, PR 00936

South Carolina

Medical University of South Carolina
Physical Therapy Program
171 Ashley Avenue
Charleston, SC 29425

Tennessee

University of Tennessee
Department of Physical Therapy
Center for Health Sciences
822 Beale Street, 3d Floor
Memphis, TN 38163

Texas

University of Texas–Southwestern Medical Center at Dallas
Department of Physical Therapy, School of Allied Health
    Sciences
5323 Harry Hines Boulevard
Dallas, TX 75235

Texas Woman's University
School of Physical Therapy
Box 22487, TWU Station
Denton, TX 76204

U.S. Army Medical Department
Graduate Program in Physical Therapy
Academy of Health Sciences
Ft. Sam Houston, TX 78234

University of Texas Medical Branch at Galveston
Department of Physical Therapy, School of Allied Health
    Sciences
Galveston, TX 77550

Texas Tech University Health Sciences Center
Department of Physical Therapy
School of Allied Health
Lubbock, TX 79430

University of Texas Health Science Center at San Antonio
Physical Therapy Program
7703 Floyd Curl Drive
San Antonio, TX 78284

Southwest Texas State University
Physical Therapy Program
Health Science Center
San Marcos, TX 78666

Utah

University of Utah
Division of Physical Therapy, College of Health
1130 Annex, Wing B
Salt Lake City, UT 84112

Vermont

University of Vermont
Department of Physical Therapy, School of Allied Health
    Sciences
305 Rowell Building
Burlington, VT 05405

Virginia

Old Dominion University
Program in Physical Therapy, Department of Community Health
    Professions
Norfolk, VA 23529-0288

Virginia Commonwealth University
Department of Physical Therapy
Box 224, MCV-Station
Richmond, VA 23298

Washington

Eastern Washington University
Department of Physical Therapy
Mail Stop 4
Cheney, WA 99004

University of Washington
Division of Physical Therapy
Department of Rehabilitation Medicine RJ-30
Seattle, WA 98195

University of Puget Sound
Department of Physical Therapy
1500 N. Warner
Tacoma, WA 98416

West Virginia

West Virginia University Medical Center
Division of Physical Therapy
Room 1195, Health Sciences North
Morgantown, WV 26506

Wisconsin

University of Wisconsin–LaCrosse
Department of Physical Therapy
243 Cowley Hall
LaCrosse, WI 54601

University of Wisconsin–Madison
Physical Therapy Department
Medical Sciences Center
1300 University Avenue, Room 5175
Madison, WI 53706

Marquette University
Program in Physical Therapy
Walter Shroeder Complex
Milwaukee, WI 53233

Canada

McGill University
Physical Therapy Program
3654 Drummond Street
Montreal, Quebec
Canada H3G1Y5

CHAPTER 4

SPORTS PHYSICIANS

Sports physicians form the core of the field of the sports medicine professional team. Athletic trainers, physical therapists, and related personnel work under the supervision of the medical doctor. Most of them work individually with athletes while some assist sports teams. For those working with teams, the American College of Sports Medicine has developed a team physical course "to provide physicians with information on the organization of medical care for athletes, development of conditioning and training programs, and coverage of athletic events."

American Orthopaedic Society for Sports Medicine former president H. Royer Collins, M.D., warns, "We have seen sports medicine clinics popping up on every street corner . . . Many have no experience in sports medicine." He encourages properly trained and experienced physicians to take the lead in sports medicine for the benefit of athletes.

Three groups fall into the category of sports physicians—doctors of medicine (M.D.); doctors of osteopathy (D.O.) and doctors of chiropractic (D.C.). These individuals normally guide the procedures of the other sports personnel and in many situations carry the final responsibility for actions taken. Osteopaths and Chiropractors are more likely to serve in a consulting capacity to schools, teams, and sports health centers. These two professions have only recently begun to gain respect within the medical community and among the general public.

The commandments of Dr. Theodore Fox, former orthopedic surgeon for the Chicago Bears professional football team, serve as excellent guidelines for all physicians. His "Team or Sports Physician's Ten Commandments" (slightly modified) follow:

1. Sports physicians must be trained in all procedures for prevention, recognition, diagnosis, and treatment of injuries in first aid as well as knowledge of soft tissue and skeletal injuries.
2. They must personally examine and evaluate all candidates for the sport or team *prior* to their participation—to determine the individual's fitness for the game. This should include a history of all previous illnesses, accidents, and surgical procedures as well as a psychological and thorough physical examination.

The physical evaluation should include observations of any physical characteristics and defects predisposing the player to injury especially in the contact sports. The physical examination should include determination of the individual's maturity, balance, coordination, ability, stamina, and strength.

3. The physicians should know the basic fundamentals of the sports in which they are working to better understand the mechanism of the injuries occurring, as well as the injured participant and his or her problem.
4. Physicians should observe and evaluate the emotional well-being of athletes, especially young players. Is a candidate being pushed by a frustrated parent to become a superstar? Is the player made apprehensive by a parent who fears he or she may get hurt?

5. The sports staff, including the physician, should fit and select all protective gear and equipment and check it for type and quality, especially in contact sports.

6. The trainers and coaches should be instructed by the physician in the proper use of physiotherapeutic techniques used in the training room. Also, physicians are responsible for conditioning and rehabilitation exercises, such as weight training.

Physicians undertake the responsibility of the rehabilitation of injured athletes. A careful examination must precede any return to participation.

7. Doctors should advise coaches not to teach practices dangerous to themselves and their opponents. In addition, mismatches between players, especially younger ones, should not be permitted. The physicians should advise the coaches concerning problems or injuries that may occur because of heat, humidity, overwork, or fatigue.

8. The physician (or designated replacements) should be available at all times to examine injured players *as soon as possible* following the injury. This remains particularly true in collision sports where, if possible, the doctor should be on the field. Often a youngster will mask an injury to continue playing. The physician must make an assessment of the severity of an injury and take appropriate measures.

9. The physician must prevent injured players from returning to the game if there exists a reasonable doubt about their condition. In doing so they must resist all pressures from coaches, parents, alumni, and players.

10. Doctors must obtain x-rays of injuries (and other information as necessary) before judging the condition of the injury.

The importance of a sports physician to the athlete can be seen from the comments of Dave Meggyesy in his book *Out of their League* (Ramparts). Meggyesy, a successful college and professional player, recalls his negative experiences with physicians in college:

> "During my four years I accumulated a broken wrist, separations of both shoulders, an ankle that was torn up so badly it broke the arch of my foot, three brain concussions, and an arm that almost had to be amputated because of improper treatment."

When a player is injured, he or she is sent to the team physician, who is usually more concerned with getting the athlete back into action than anything else. This reversal of priorities leads to unbelievable abuses.

The entire sports medicine staff and particularly the physician has a serious obligation—careful adherence to Dr. Fox's "Ten Commandments" will curtail many of the serious medical abuses associated with athletics.

DOCTOR OF MEDICINE

Over 400,000 active medical doctors practice in the nation today. Most have obtained advanced training in a specialty. Some general practitioners (G.P.s) have served as team physicians on the local level. For example, Dr. George Freyburger served as the physician to the Weehawken (New Jersey) public schools. This assignment involved regular general physical examinations for all students, special projects that might result from student illnesses, and sports teams physician. In addition, he maintained a private office practice. However, most doctors of medicine involved in sports have their training as orthopedists.

Orthopedists

Orthopedists treat injuries to the skeletal system—backs, necks, arms, legs, and joints—and to the body's muscles. They utilize a wide range of techniques to restore the athlete to full capacity to return to action.

They usually work long days, but their salaries are excellent; yearly incomes of $200,000 are not uncommon. Orthopedist Philip J. Mayer, M.D., describes his typical day:

> "I generally make early morning rounds at the hospital between eight and nine o'clock and then on out-patient days I start at nine o'clock and work right through the day, finishing with out-patients at approximately 5:30. We try to fit in a 15 or 20 minute break in the middle of the afternoon. On an operative day, we will start in the operating room at 7:30 and try to have our last case out of the operating room by 3:30 in the afternoon. Unfortunately, sometimes we do run over and late hours are quite typical."

Presently Dr. Mayer serves on the staff of the Department of Orthopaedics, School of Medicine of the State University of New York at Stony Brook. A pioneer in sports medicine on Long Island, he presently works with the university's sports teams, sees athletes referred from GPs and works with the general public as well.

Dr. Vincent Di Stefano, the team physician for the Philadelphia Eagles professional football team, likewise maintains a busy schedule. This orthopedist not only services the Eagles but serves as president of Sports Orthopaedists and works with the Graduate Hospital—Human Performance and Sports Medicine Center in Wayne, Pennsylvania. He sees athletes on referral from physicians, works with the general public, and finally manages to find time to write articles for sports medicine journals.

A certain strong obligation exists among sports medicine professionals to improve their procedures. Many physicians conduct clinical research while others pursue experimental studies. The following examples characterize the type of research underway: The Use of Anti-Inflamatory Drugs in the Treatment of Sports Injuries, Lyle Micheli, M.D., director, Division of Sports Medicine, Children's Hospital Medical Center, Boston; Anorexia Nervosa and Bulimia in Dancers, Michelle Warren, M.D., director of Reproductive Endocrinology, St. Luke's Roosevelt Hospital, New York City; Amenorrhea: Not for Athletes Only, Chung H. Su, M.D., professor of Obstetrics and Gynecology at Jefferson Medical College, Philadelphia; Chemical Warfare: Drugs in Sports, Edward Percy, M.D., director, Sports Medicine Program and associate professor, Department of Surgery, University of Arizona.

The career's rewards are numerous, but preparing for the job is demanding.

Education Requirements

Admission to medical school remains very difficult. Many people begin to think of attending while still in high school and plan their courses accordingly by taking college preparatory courses with a strong emphasis in science. Not only must potential candidates do well academically but perform well on the Medical College Admissions Test (MCAT). This test attempts to evaluate the student's potential for success in medical school. In the United States there exist 126 accredited medical schools. Following graduation, a residency in a specialty is undertaken; at this point the individual receives a modest salary. Those interested in sports medicine most likely would pursue an orthopedic residency of from two to five years. All states, the District of Columbia, and Puerto Rico require a license to practice medicine; successful completion of the licensing exam is necessary.

A variety of interesting career opportunities exists for the orthopedist in sports medicine. The future will see continued growth in job options, personal satisfaction, and salary.

Additional information concerning medical doctors may be obtained from the following:

American Medical Association
535 North Dearborn Street
Chicago, IL 60610

Association of American Medical Colleges
One Du Pont Circle, N.W.
Washington, DC 20036

American Orthopaedic Society for Sports Medicine
70 West Hubbard Street, Suite 202
Chicago, IL 60610

Council on Medical Education
American Medical Association
(see address above)

DOCTOR OF OSTEOPATHY

Hearing a patient say, ''I feel great—you helped me'' is what makes life enjoyable for William Previte, D.O. Previte, a San Diego-based physician, concentrates most of his practice on sports medicine. ''I love working with active, motivated people who heal well and want to return to action. I feel an immediate reward—as I help players to return to active participation in their sports. I don't deal with death and dying.'' Previte's comments reflect the reasons why many people in the sports medicine field have chosen their career. Following graduation from Philadelphia College of Osteopathic Medicine, he undertook a series of residencies, including a fellowship with Dr. James Andrews, an internationally famous orthopaedic surgeon. He later relocated to the San Diego area, which features a very active life-style among its people.

Some individuals interested in medicine choose the osteopathic path because of its traditional emphasis on the muscular-skeletal system of the body—bones, muscles, ligaments, and nerves. Osteopaths offer their patients an additional type of health care— manipulation. That is, one of the basic treatments of osteopathy involving the use of the hands in manipulative procedures and therapy. As do medical doctors, osteopaths use surgery, drugs, and other accepted health care practices.

There exist over 20,000 osteopathic physicians in the United States. The profession will expand greatly in the next twenty years, doubling its membership. Most D.O.s enter general practice as family physicians, setting up private offices. This is somewhat consistent with osteopathy, as it aims to treat the whole person. Those specializing in sports medicine would therefore be more likely to consider the total health of the person in treating an injury.

Education

Presently, fourteen colleges of osteopathic medicine exist in the United States. The curriculum matches that of medical doctors in many ways; typical courses include anatomy, physiology, chemistry, pathology, bacteriology, immunology, and pharmacology. In addition, course work is spent on the oneness of the body's system and osteopathic manipulation.

A strong background in science in high school and college remains a must; most physicians have taken undergraduate college majors in biology. One osteopath offers this advice: "While in undergraduate school, major in biology or premed, take athletic training courses as electives if possible, gain an exposure to all the sciences, and attend talks by doctors and others on sports medicine."

Osteopathy and the osteopathic colleges have fought a long battle to gain acceptance from M.D.s and from the public. They have been somewhat but not totally successful. The opportunities in sports medicine for doctors of osteopathy will be better than those in other osteopathic specialties; income will likewise reflect this. Most osteopaths do well financially (approximately $40,000 per year) but, on the average, not as well as M.D.s.

As with M.D.s, osteopaths undertake residencies upon graduation; for those interested in sports medicine, the residency will take from three to five years. Following this period most will become certified as orthopedic surgeons. Regardless of specialty, all D.O.s must obtain licensing in all states.

For those interested in sports medicine, osteopathy deserves their serious consideration as a career choice; for additional information contact:

American Association of Osteopathic Medicine
4720 Montgomery Lane
Washington, DC 20014

American Osteopathic Association
212 East Ohio Street
Chicago, IL 60611

DOCTOR OF CHIROPRACTIC

Mike Billauer, D.C., maintains his office in Marina Del Rey, California, where he specializes in working with athletes. He has served as team physician for the U.S. men's volleyball team for the 1988 Olympics and has traveled with the team to the other international matches in Cuba and the Soviet Union. He believes "an athlete can perform best where their neuromuscular–skeletal system is functioning at its optimum level—in perfect balance." Billauer, a graduate of Queens College (New York) and Los Angeles College of Chiropractic (Whittier, California), believes his is the greatest profession in the world. "We help people by natural means—chiropractors have long been in the vanguard of 'say no to drugs.'"

Chiropractic physicians emphasize the utilization of manipulation (adjustments) as their primary treatment. They believe that a person's (in this case the athlete's) health to a large degree relates to the welfare of the nervous system. Interference with this system impairs normal function and lowers resistance to disease. D.C.s generally work with the spine to restore proper functioning to the nervous system. In addition to manipulation they utilize water, light, massage, ultrasound, and electric and heat therapy. Often they prescribe a special diet, nutritional supplements, exercise, and rest to heal the injured athlete. They do not believe in using prescription drugs or surgery as part of their approach nor are they permitted by the state in which they practice to do this.

More than 30,000 licensed chiropractors practice their profession in the United States. Most have a private office, and others work at clinics and chiropractic colleges where they engage in teaching and research. Those engaged in sports medicine usually make it known that they emphasize the treatment of athletes. Some teams maintain a chiropractor as a consultant should they need her or his services.

Education

High school course work in the college preparatory or academic program with a strong emphasis in science provides a good background for the future chiropractor. Chiropractic colleges require two years of college prior to admission; some students have their college degrees. In two years of general college students must take English; psychology; social sciences and humanities; biological sciences including laboratory; chemistry (organic, inorganic) with a laboratory; and physics.

At chiropractic colleges, students pursue a program featuring anatomy, biochemistry, microbiology, pathology, physiology, public health, diagnosis, x-ray, related health sciences, chiropractic principles and practices, and clinical experience. Be aware that not all chiropractic colleges have received accreditation of the Council on Chiropractic Education. Contact the council or the associations at the end of this section for a list of accredited schools.

Licensing standards for state approval of chiropractors vary. Some states require the passage of the Basic Science Board Examination in addition to the examination of the National Board of Chiropractic Examiners.

Chiropractic medicine will continue to expand and gain respectability as the nation's interest in holistic approaches to health continues to advance. Holistic medicine's emphasis on prevention and de-emphasis of drug therapy meshes nicely with the philosophy of chiropractic.

A strong interest in sports medicine exists among chiropractors. In addition, some former athletes have entered the profession: Dr. Fred Cox, former placekicker for the Minnesota Vikings professional football team, is now a D.C., and another football player, Denver Bronco Jack Doblin, in the off-season attends chiropractic college. Within the profession, an organization exists for those interested in the treatment of athletes: the Council on Sports Injuries (see address below).

The expansion and acceptance of chiropractic medicine will result in continued salary improvements. Salaries currently range from $40,000 to $75,000 per year.

If this profession interests you contact:

American Chiropractic Association
1701 Clarendon Boulevard
Arlington, VA 22209

International Chiropractors Association
1110 Glebe Road
Arlington, VA 22201

Council on Chiropractic Education
3209 Ingersoll Avenue
Des Moines, IA 50312

Council on Sports Injuries
American Chiropractic Association
(address above)

The following books will be helpful to those considering careers in any of the three sports physician areas:

ACSM's Guidelines for Health and Fitness Facilities. Human Kinetics Publishers, P.O. Box 5076, Champaign, IL 61825.

ACSM's Guidelines for the Team Physician. Lee and Febiger Publishers, Malvern, PA 19355.

ACSM's Healthy Exercise. Human Kinetics Publishers, P.O. Box 5076, Champaign, IL 61825.

Chiropractic. Chiropractic Education Commission, American Chiropractic Association.

For the Practitioner: Orthopaedic Screening Examination for Participation in Sports. Ross Laboratories, Columbus, OH 43216.

Health Care for the Female Athlete. The Athletic Institute, 200 N. Castlewood Drive, North Palm Beach, FL 33408.

Helping Hands: Challenge of Medicine; Helping Hands: Financing a Health Career; Helping Hands: Horizons Unlimited in Medicine; Helping Hands: A Selected Bibliography of Financial Aid for, and Health Careers. Order Department, American Medical Association, P.O. Box 821, Monroe, WI 53566.

Medicine—A Woman's Career. American Medical Women's Association, 1740 Broadway, New York, NY 10019.

Opportunities in Physician Careers—VGM Career Horizons, National Textbook Co., 4255 W. Touhy Avenue, Lincolnwood, IL 60646.

Osteopathic Medicine. Department of Public Relations, American Osteopathic Association, 212 East Ohio Street, Chicago, IL 60611.

Sports Health (The Complete Book of Athletic Injuries). The Athletic Institute, 200 N. Castlewood Drive, North Palm Beach, FL 33408.

Sports Medicine for the Athletic Female. Medical Economics, Oradell, NJ.

200 Ways to Put Your Talent to Work in the Health Field. National Health Council, 1740 Broadway, New York, NY 10019.

The Young Athlete's Health Handbook. The Athletic Institute, 200 N. Castlewood Drive, North Palm Beach, FL 33408.

CHAPTER 5

OTHER SPORTS MEDICINE CAREERS

STRENGTH AND CONDITIONING SPECIALIST

All athletes and sports enthusiasts realize the value of conditioning and strength training. But proper conditioning and training is a lot more than pumping iron. Today, the athlete's training program must be sports specific. That is, a tennis player must develop different muscles and endurance than a professional football lineman.

The professional organization that certifies individuals in this sports medicine specialty is the National Strength and Conditioning Association (NSCA), with approximately 15,000 members. The suggestions for training in this association's excellent journals reflect the most recent scientific research. For example, its *Journal of Applied Sports Science Research* in a recent issue contained articles entitled "Effects of Weighted Implement Training on Throwing Velocity," "Assessing Anaerobic Power in Collegiate Football Players," and "Applications of Electrostimulation in Physical Conditioning: A Review." Another of its periodicals, the *National Strength and Conditioning Association Journal,* contains articles on "Diving: Upper Body Strength and Conditioning for

Divers,'' ''Off-season Strength Training' for Basketball,'' and ''The Science of Cross-training: Theory and Application for Peak Performance.'' In addition, the NSCA provides videotapes, conferences, posters, courses, and checklists which are beneficial to the membership. Perhaps its most valuable contribution to the profession is its program to certify specialists in the field. Certification includes the right to be designated as a CSCS (certified strength and conditioning specialist).

Specialists in strength and conditioning normally work for professional and college teams; some work directly with athletes on a consulting basis. Often a sports medicine center or a health and fitness club will utilize the services of these specialists on a part-time basis. This career field will continue to grow as athletes (and the general public) continue to increase their desire for athletic success enhanced by strength training and physical conditioning.

While certification does require as one of its criteria a college degree, some people work successfully without the benefit of a college diploma. These individuals have acquired through study and experience a knowledge of the field. However, specialists in the future will need a college degree to find employment. Few will be hired without certification.

For additional information contact:

The National Strength and Conditioning Association
P.O. Box 81410
Lincoln, NE 68504

PODIATRY

It's a rare sport that does not put great strain on the participant's feet. For the estimated 80 percent of all people who have foot problems, even minor ones, the increase of physical activity can cause even greater difficulties.

These difficulties normally lead the injured party to the office of a podiatrist. These health professionals, usually identified by the initials D.P.M. (doctor of podiatric medicine), specialize in the care of healthy feet. Utilizing medical, surgical, and physical techniques, they work to prevent or treat foot injuries and diseases.

Richard Berenter, D.P.M., M.S., typifies the background of most podiatrists. He received his bachelor's of science degree with a specialty in zoology from the University of Maryland and four years later graduated from the California college of Podiatric Medicine (CCPM). He then completed additional postgraduate study and residencies. He presently serves on the faculty of CCPM, works in the college biomechanical laboratories, and collaborates with the staff of St. Francis Hospital Center for Sports Medicine. He has done considerable work with athletes and runners. Like his fellow sports medicine professionals, he loves his career because ''he makes a difference.''

Most podiatrists have their own offices. Others work in hospitals and group situations such as sport clinics. Working conditions are enjoyable and salaries are very good. As with other health professionals, a strong interest in science and people remains important. Likewise, good health and an inclination toward academic learning is important because of the long period of education and training required.

Podiatry and Sports

The growing interest in sports medicine has not escaped those medical personnel concerned with proper foot care. In fact, the escalating number of sports injuries to the lower extremities forced podiatrists to become more involved with athletics.

Consequently, a group of professionals founded the American Academy of Podiatric Sports Medicine (AAPSM) in 1970. This organization engages in a number of activities for the benefit of its membership. It promotes and collects research on podiatric sports medicine—what procedures help prevent injuries and promote rehabilitation. The academy offers a yearly seminar covering topics such as psychological aspects of sports rehabilitation, children's lower extremity sports injuries, and sports medicine in the 1990s. A professional magazine serves to keep members informed.

Presently, colleges for the education of sports podiatry do not exist. Students interested in this field must attend one of the colleges of podiatric medicine and then apply for membership in the AAPSM. The organization has three categories of membership—fellows, associate members, and honorary members. Candidates for associate membership must have a degree from and accredited institution of higher education, and, if a podiatrist, membership in the American Podiatric Association is required. For the prestigious position of fellow, the individual must earn a doctorate in one of the following areas: podiatric medicine, medicine, osteopathy, dentistry, education, philosophy, physical education, public health, or a related area. Secondly, the candidate must have attended one of the meetings of AAPSM. Third, the individual must have served as a team physician or team podiatrist for a minimum of two years. Fourth, the candidate has to show evidence of five years of professional experience in the prevention and treatment of sports injuries or must have published two or more articles on sports medicine topics. Fifth, an original publishable article on a sports medicine topic is required. Finally, the candidate takes a comprehensive written and oral exam. Successful completion of all requirements results in admission to the academy as a fellow. This carries with it both prestige and financial rewards.

Sports podiatry is quickly becoming one of the most exciting and rapidly growing fields within podiatry and generally within sports medicine. Dr. Lee Cohen, D.P.M., of Morton, Pennsylvania, has developed a Cushioned Anti-Pronation Insert (CAPI) for athletes. The device serves as a shock absorber and is part of Dr. Cohen's preventative approach to sports medicine. He states, ''It's no fun to see 40 or 50 people a day complaining of pain. It's more efficient to take some preventative steps ahead of time.'' Cohen further believes that ''we need to make the change from sports medicine to sports-injury prevention.''

Dr. Cohen developed CAPI as a result of videotaping athletes during their performance at Springfield High School in Delaware County, Pennsylvania. In studying the videotape, he found which part of the foot needed support depending upon its use in the contest. Different sports place different demands upon the foot. In the short time Cohen has served his profession, he has had the opportunity to contribute to the success of many athletes, making for a personally rewarding career.

Dr. Ron Valmassy, D.P.M., head of the department of biomechanics, California College of Podiatric Medicine, believes that ''podiatry is a great field if one is interested in medicine in general with a particular interest in sports. We are in the forefront of treating numerous types of foot and leg problems that plague both the recreational and professional athlete.''

Additional information about this profession may be obtained from:

American Academy of Podiatric Sports Medicine
1729 Glastonberry Road
Potomac, MD 20854

Colleges of podiatric medicine are:

California College of Podiatric Medicine
Box 7855
Rincon Annex
San Francisco, CA 94120

College of Podiatric Medicine and Surgery
University of Osteopathic Medicine and Health Sciences
3200 Grand Avenue
Des Moines, IA 50312

College of Podiatric Medicine
1001 N. Dearborn Avenue
Chicago, IL 60610

Pennsylvania College of Podiatric Medicine
Eighth and Race Streets
Philadelphia, PA 19107

SPORTS PROSTHETICS AND ORTHOTICS

National Hockey League players Brian Trottier and Mike McEwen had a problem. They suffered from elbow hyperextension, a not uncommon problem faced by hockey skaters resulting from the strain placed on the joint by their slap shot.

They contacted Andy Myers, a specialist in prosthetics and orthotics. Myers serves as director of Prosthetics and Orthotics Services, located in West Hempstead, Long Island, in New York State. He designed a brace to control the extension of the elbow; they used it extensively in practice and occasionally in games. Their elbow problem was significantly controlled.

What are prosthetics and orthotics? These two related sciences, while frequently linked together, involve separate specialties. The utilization of artificial replacement limbs characterizes prosthetics while the use of bracing to correct and support a body part falls into the field of orthotics. Orthotics would be more likely to be applied to the problems of athletes. However, there exists a growing number of handicapped people successfully participating in sports. It would not be unusual for a prosthetic specialist to design a limb to enable an athlete to participate in gymnastics or football.

Andy Myers, although certified in both areas, concentrates his efforts in orthotics, and within this field his sub-specialties include pediatrics, sports medicine, and spinal deformities. For example, one device he has constructed to assist athletes is the body jacket (known in the profession as an anterior flexiform spinal orthosis). Myers has used the jacket to treat football linemen and gymnasts for a fracture of the vertebrae of the spine. This injury is common to those types of athletes because of the stress and impact they put on their back and spine. The body jacket has enabled these people to return to practice and competition.

Myers, typical of the young people that have entered the field, graduated from the program of prosthetics and orthotics from New York University. Following placement in the field working under the supervision of a certified professional for one year each in prosthetics and orthotics, he took his examinations to become certified. Satisfactory completion of these comprehensive tests qualify the person as certified, with the designation C.P.O. Now the individual can engage in the profession.

Andy Myers is very enthusiastic about the future of his chosen career. "It is a growing field, filled with new techniques and innovation." For example, Myers sees the development of new materials as exciting. "Sorbothane, a shock-absorbing and dispersing material, is something we now utilize in football equipment and within runners' shoes." Myers, who is completing his doctoral thesis in the field of biomechanics studying rotator cuff injuries, enjoys working with serious athletes. "These are healthy, well-tuned people with a specific disability. The challenge becomes how to prevent, to support, or to correct while not interfering with the performance.'' Like his fellow professionals, Andy Myers works with the injured part-time or weekend athlete. Here he sees his objective ''as helping them to return to their livelihood as soon as possible.''

One development that makes the field of orthotics and prosthetics of expanding interest as a career is the growing respect it has received from the sports medicine community. Orthopedists often consult with orthotists regarding developments before they recommend treatment for a patient. Athletes now realize the value of orthotic devices to their successful performance, whereas, in previous decades, they would resist this inconvenience.

A good example of the growing respect orthotics has gained is reflected in a recent article in *The First Aider Magazine* entitled ''Orthotics May Help Ease Knee Pain'' by Ronald Valmassy, D.P.M. Dr. Valmassy suggests that in some knee cases a ''prescription type of in-shoe orthotic is often useful in alleviating chronic or recurrent symptoms.''

Andy Myers states that ''in today's team approach in sports medicine, doctors are willing to utilize competently trained allied health personnel such as orthotists and prosthetists.'' Clearly these careers will be among the most exciting of any in the years ahead.

A growing number of schools have begun to offer programs to train people in the field of prosthetics and orthotics. New York University's Department of Prosthetics and Orthotics offers short-term courses for a variety of health professionals as well as a two-year certificate program and a four-year bachelor of science program.

Students in these programs take courses such as Above-knee Prosthetics, which has the following course description: ''Includes lectures, demonstrations, and laboratory exercises in stump casting, cast modification, socket fabrication, static and dynamic alignment, alignment duplication, and suspension systems, supplemented by basic information on anatomy, normal locomotion and biomechanics.'' Those enrolled in the NYU bachelor's degree program take a regular college curriculum in addition to specialized courses such as Biomechanics, Spinal Orthotics, Survey of Orthopedic and Neuromuscular Conditions, and Professional Problems in Prosthetics and Orthotics. As with all medical training, the student has a clinical experience—serving an internship at prosthetics and orthotics facilities. The graduate must then successfully pass an examination in prosthetics and/or orthotics to obtain certification.

If this field appeals to you, you may wish to contact the following organization for additional information:

The American Orthotic and Prosthetic Association
717 Pendleton Street
Alexandria, VA 22314

Additionally, the following institutions offer educational programs.

California

Rancho Los Amigos Hospital
Orthotic Department (orthotics only)
7450 Leeds Street
Downey, CA 90242

University of California at Los Angeles
Department of Orthotics and Prosthetics
1000 Vetran Avenue
Los Angeles, CA 90024

Illinois

Northwestern University Medical School
Prosthetic Orthotic Center
345 East Superior Street
Chicago, IL 60611

Massachusetts

NOPCO/CETA Skills Center
11 Hayward Street
Quincy, MA 02171

Minnesota

916 Area Vocational Technical Institute
3300 Century Avenue North
White Bear Lake, MN 55110

New York

New York University Medical School
Department of Prosthetics and Orthotics
317 East 34th Street
New York, NY 10016

Tennessee

Shelby State Community College
P.O. Box 4568
Memphis, TN 38104

Texas

University of Texas
School of Allied Health Sciences
5328 Harry Hines Boulevard
Dallas, TX 75235

Washington

University of Washington
School of Medicine
Division of Prosthetics and Orthotics
Seattle, WA 98195

SPORTS NUTRITIONIST

Recent Developments

For centuries those engaged in athletics looked for "the edge"—that something that would enable them to produce an excellent competitive performance. This pursuit usually centered on conditioning and durability and more recently on weight training, stretching, and mental toughness.

A few athletes looked to the relationship between nutritional supplementation and athletic performance. The first major research development occurred in the 1960s at the University of Illinois when Dr. Thomas Cureton found that a constituent of wheat germ oil improved athletic performance. Some athletes, largely those in track and field, began to supplement their diets with raw wheat germ and the oil in capsules. In 1972, Cureton published the book *The Physiological Effects of Wheat Germ Oil on Humans in Exercise,* in which he shared his research on the contribution of wheat germ to athletic performance.

It took several years for the next breakthroughs. Rumors began to leak from the Soviet Union and the Scandinavian countries that their athletes utilized nutrients that aided their performances. Following some sensational successes in the Olympics, interest heightened.

More recently, some positive results from scientific studies have resulted in an expanded interest by athletes in what to eat, when to eat, what supplements (minerals, vitamins, herbs) to use, and how to utilize them properly. Unfortunately, some supplement producers have exaggerated the effects of their products, and when this was detected, athletes and the public were confused. Despite such setbacks, the nutrition movement continues to gain adherents, as research shows positive results for the importance of diet to injury prevention and optimum performance. Additionally, as studies in the United States and abroad show enhanced athletic performance due to substances such as ginseng, chromium picolinate, octocosonol, and germanium, players will continue to look for guidance in this area.

Sports Nutrition Careers

The advances in nutrition and the growing realization of its value by the public, the medical establishment, and the sports establishment will catapult sports nutritionists into a major role in the years ahead.

Most nutritionists involved in sports serve in a consulting capacity with coaches, teams, and individual athletes. They offer suggestions regarding weight control, pregame meals, and vitamin-mineral supplementation.

Professional sports nutritionists may have backgrounds and education in either medicine or nutrition; some may also have obtained their training as dieticians, nurses, athletic trainers, and physical therapists. Through additional study and reading, these individuals have prepared themselves to serve the sports community as nutritionists. For example, Jim Corea, Ph.D., R.P.T., a physical therapist, undertook additional college studies in nutrition in graduate school. He presently offers advice at his gym in

Cherry Hill, New Jersey, his office in Moorestown, New Jersey, and on his daily radio program on WWDB-FM in Philadelphia.

One individual in this field, Dr. Sarah Short, Ph.D., Ed.D., R.D., professor of nutrition at Syracuse University, has an interest in computerized sports nutrition. Dr. Short has investigated the nutrition requirements of various athletes (football players, wrestlers, swimmers, and others) in terms of protein, calories, minerals, vitamins, and other nutrients. She hopes to call attention to the importance of the nutritional needs of athletes. The increase of such attention to sports nutrition will undoubtedly encourage allied health personnel to gravitate to the field of nutrition.

Some medical schools offer medical degrees with a specialty in nutrition, and many additional graduate schools provide doctorates. For those not wishing advanced study, some schools of allied health science offer a bachelor's degree in nutrition. A strong background and interest in science is important for this career as well as openness to new developments in the field. The growing prestige of the position of the nutrition specialist and its importance among the public generally and among athletes specifically makes this an attractive career.

For additional information read *Sports Nutrition* (Keats Publishing, New Canaan, Connecticut) by Walter Evans and *Optimum Nutrition for Athletes* (Morrow Publisher, New York) by Michael Colgan; subscribe to *Nutrition and Fitness*, 511 Encinitas Boulevard, Suite 101, Encinitas, CA 90024 and write to:

International Center for Sports Nutrition
502 South 44th Street
Suite 3012
Omaha, NE 68105

SPORTS VISION CAREERS

Today's orientation in eye care for athletes goes beyond the basics to vision enhancement. The subtitle of a book on the topic reflects this emphasis: *The Athletic Eye—Improved Sports Performance through Visual Training*. Several new companies have begun to provide equipment designed to improve the vision of athletes relative to the visual demands of their sport and the position they play. Unfortunately, despite such advances, few members of the athletic community avail themselves of these methods.

In complaining about the lack of attention given to optic care, a Dallas Cowboys trainer states, "The eyes are probably the last phase deemed important in sports medicine." Although in the early stages of development, sports vision is ready to make a major contribution in the area of athletics.

The Dallas Cowboys football team, always a leader in utilizing new techniques to maximize player effectiveness, has instituted a program in sports vision. Dr. Burt Fisher, an optometrist who assists the team, has treated a number of players and evaluates all the rookies. Bausch and Lomb's Council on Sports Vision has discovered these early warning signs for detection of vision problems:

- athletes who squint to see clearly
- football players who have difficulty seeing the ball and catching passes
- tennis players who have difficulty focusing on the ball and reacting to the serve
- golfers who have trouble discerning the distance to the green
- basketball players who are uncertain in their ball handling, miss too many free shots, or tend to close one eye when they shoot

- athletes who constantly rub their eyes or suffer from headaches or excessive tearing

Dr. Don Getz, president of the Sports Vision Systems of the World Sports Council, has conducted extensive research on athletes. Getz believes the successful athlete has a greater "reaction system." "We take the attitude that the vision system directs the muscular system. That determines their athletic ability," states Getz. Is his approach successful? "After a few months with us, we can lift a baseball player's batting average by 50 points. I'd say 100, but people don't believe me," claimed Dr. Getz of Van Nuys, California.

While most of the public, including athletes, remain unaware of the dynamic value of vision therapy, Steven DeVore and Greggory DeVore, M.D., have had excellent results working with a variety of athletes. The DeVore brothers' technique, called *sybervision,* lists a number of successes; a few examples follow:

> At California State University at Hayward, two of the lowest ranking tennis players tried the technique. The results made international news. Their coach commented, 'In all my years of coaching I have never seen such rapid progress in athletes before.

> Doug True, who played on the University of California basketball team, utilized the system to improve his shooting percentage; he was drafted by the Phoenix Suns of the National Basketball Association.

> Numerous supportive commentaries exist. Dr. Sarah Jaque, a medical physicist and specialist in physiology at Hebrew University stated, 'Individuals trained in Syber-vision skills will have a sharper mental discipline, refined performance skills and a quicker reaction time.' Dr. Richard Scavone, Stanford University sports psychologist and an Olympic coach states: 'Syber-vision is one of the most concrete, theoretically sound, strongest programs of sports

performance development and improvement in existence today.'

Clearly this training system will attract more and more athletes, and additional sports optometrists (and optometric assistants and technicians) will be necessary to implement this program and others.

For those thinking of a career in a sports-related profession, one of the most exciting and rewarding will be in sports vision. Recently, Dr. Burt Fisher lamented, "It seems odd that parents and coaches will spend so much time developing a young athlete and so much money purchasing the necessary equipment and padding and then ignore proper eye care." Fortunately the message of Dr. Fisher and his fellow sports vision specialists has begun to attract attention; future players in all sports at all levels will include serious attention to this aspect of human performance.

As with other medical personnel, the education and training of ophthalmologists (M.D.s) and optometrists (D.O.s) requires a serious commitment and long study. An interest in science and academics generally exists as an important criterion for success. Interested persons should consult the VGM Career Horizons series books entitled *Opportunities in Optometry* and *Opportunities in Eye Care Careers.*

The professional organization of optometrists may be contacted at:

American Optometric Association
243 North Lindbergh Boulevard
St. Louis, MO 63141

The Professional Society of Ophthalmologists may be contacted at:

American Academy of Ophthalmology
655 Beach Street
San Francisco, CA 94109

SPORTS DENTISTRY

When I've tried pitching without the mouthguard I get
tired quicker and feel more pain in my arm afterwards. Some
might say it's psychological, but I don't think so.
                                    Hank Iervolino
                                    Former Baseball Pitcher
                                    New York Technological University

One of the areas of sports medicine that has created excitement
in recent years has been the use of special mouthpieces. Interest
in these devices skyrocketed following a *Sports Illustrated* report.
Technically called a mandibular orthopedic repositioning application (MORA), this dental apparatus fits over the lower teeth and
readjusts the malalignment from which many athletes suffer.
Some players reported increased overall performance and particularly improved strength. Dr. Richard Kaufman, a Long Island,
New York, orthodontist, a pioneer in this field, believes, ''It is
essential to place the jaw in a proper position to enable the athlete
to function at his maximum potential capacity.'' Kaufman further
states, ''I have been conducting tests to show that injuries can be
reduced and overall physical functioning can be increased by
using a custom-fitted mouthpiece which places the jaw in optimum position.'' While not all research agrees with Kaufman,
there exists general agreement that the position of the jaw has
much to do with total body energy and muscle strength. Additional research is presently being conducted to validate the effectiveness of the MORA. Undoubtedly for some individuals this
device will have a beneficial effect.

Clearly for dentists with an interest in sports, the ongoing development of special mouth devices makes this a very exciting career.

Naturally dentists serve athletes in many traditional ways. Many dentists work with players to help them avoid injury to the mouth area through the use of dental devices if necessary and other protection such as face guards in football. The utilization of the mouthpiece and face guard has cut injuries by 60 percent. Dentists provide regular dental examinations; nothing will "bench" an athlete faster than an abscessed tooth. In case of injury to the mouth, the dentist provides appropriate treatment.

Few, if any, dentists involve themselves with sports on a full-time basis. In addition to their regular practice, some dentists serve athletic teams as consultants. They are paid a yearly fee for their duties relating to the team. Others volunteer their services to school and community teams.

The American Dental Association (ADA) has outlined the general primary functions of the team dentist:

1. The dentist is responsible for making sure that players have good oral health at the start of the season.
2. The team dentist helps set up and implement the school mouth protector program. Each year, the dentist and school officials should discuss when the program should take place, how and by whom it will be run, what kind of protectors should be used, and what the costs will be.
3. The team dentist can treat emergency dental problems if the player's own dentist is not available or can administer first aid if the team physician is not present.

The ADA provides additional suggestions, guidelines, and information to dentists to assist them in this highly specialized area.

Lawrence Kerr, D.D.S., chairman, Committee on Dental Health, United States Olympic Committee's Sports Medicine

Council, feels he and the organization serve athletes and athletics in four ways. First, they serve in an educational fashion by helping athletes realize that total health includes dental fitness. A recent development has been the requirement that women participating in field hockey must wear a mouthpiece when playing under the auspices of the U.S. Olympic Committee. Dr. Kerr and his committee hope that this requirement will have an educational effect by trickling down to the college and high school levels. Second, the committee on dental health screens athletes prior to international competition. In some cases the treatment of an infected tooth has resulted in dramatic improvement in the athlete's performance. Third, the committee provides remedial care and aids the athlete in securing dental care at his or her hometown. The committee has prepared a national list of dentists with an interest in and appropriate skills for working with athletes. The committee stands available to assist fans at major international athletic contests with remedial care. Fourth, the Dental Health Committee conducts and fosters research such as the experiments conducted on the value of the MORA.

Dental care should be part of the total training program of every athlete and every athletic team. Fortunately, coaches and players have realized this; in the future many opportunities will exist for the dentist interested in sports medicine.

The education of a dentist is a long, arduous process. It requires excellent academic performance in high school, college, and dental school. However, the rewards are great. Sports dentistry can provide the opportunity to work with athletes on an ongoing basis and for those interested, the chance to invent and develop dental devices contributing to increased athletic performance.

Additional information about dentistry can be found in *Opportunities in Dental Care Careers* (VGM Career Horizons series) and on sports dentistry from:

American Dental Association
211 East Chicago Avenue
Chicago, IL 60611

EXERCISE AND FITNESS CAREERS

Aerobics instructor, exercise physiologist, health club employee, corporate fitness director, human performance laboratory assistant/technician, fitness equipment designer/salesperson—all fall into the category of exercise and fitness careers. For a prospective member of these careers, this is great. It permits the candidate to select a sophisticated career requiring rigorous academic training (for a master's degree or doctorate) or a less complex one requiring a high school degree and a weekend certification workshop.

Marilee Matheney serves as the director of fitness at one of the nation's finest health club facilities, Shiley Sports and Health Center of Scripps Center (La Jolla, California). "I knew as a high school student that I wanted to get into fitness and sports medicine; in college I knew I wanted to be on the preventive side," states Matheney. She now lives out her career fantasy and does so by helping people. In preparing for her career, Marilee received her bachelor's degree from Texas A. & M. University in biology and received her master's in exercise physiology and health and fitness management.

Heading the movement to maximize athletic performance are exercise physiologists. Those involved in athletics normally work at sports centers serving the following major functions—assisting serious and weekend athletes to achieve fitness; developing conditioning and injury prevention programs for teams with coaches and other sports medicine personnel; evaluating the potential of athletes; helping to recover from injury; and, probably the most publicized, working with world class athletes to improve their performances.

The underlying assumption of exercise physiologists (who most often work closely with a variety of other sports medicine professionals) is that through analysis of the elements of athletic prowess, they will be able to teach athletes to perform even better. Consequently, across the nation and the world, new research continues to provide innovative methods of evaluating performance and training techniques.

Exercise physiologists utilize modern technology to complete their tasks. The combination of slow motion films, videotapes, and computers gives clues for perfecting performance. For example, by using a biomechanical computer analyzing the placement of the joints of the body, scientists have discovered that keeping the feet flat against the ground throughout the entire throwing motion will yield the greatest distance for the javelin thrower.

In analyzing performance, Dr. Marvin Clein, founder and director of the University of Denver Human Performance Laboratory, explains some of his procedures: "The first thing you look at when you test an athlete is the ability to use oxygen." Clein states that the physical capacity to deliver a powerful explosive force (arm power or leg power) serves as an important prerequisite. The laboratory looks at other aspects of the athlete's physiology—bowed legs assist football running backs, fast-twitch muscle fiber react well to quick-moving, high-intensity sports, narrow hips enable long distance runners to amass medals.

Some human performance laboratories work with the public as well as athletes. For example, the fine Sports Science Laboratory at the University of Delaware, perhaps best known for its research on world-class ice skaters, has utilized its "motion analysis system" (a series of video cameras and computers) and its other technology to analyze fire fighters' boots. The results found a new, lighter, specially constructed leather boot of greater benefit than traditional rubber ones. It has become more and more common for the benefits of sports medicine to extend beyond the athlete. The human performance laboratories employ a full range of sports medicine professionals; normally, however, exercise physiologists are paramount.

This career remains wide open for employment for those interested in the sports aspects of the work of exercise physiologists. The preparation of these professionals normally requires the completion of a master's degree, and many complete the doctorate. Frequently the undergraduate college education of exercise physiologists has taken place in a sports-related area such as athletic training or physical education. Many universities with an interest in sports medicine prepare exercise physiologists through interdisciplinary course work with a strong science emphasis. For example, graduate students in the Sport, Leisure and Exercise Sciences program at the University of Connecticut take courses such as the following: Sport for the Disabled—An Analysis of the Current Literature as It Applies to Sport and Recreational Programs for the Disabled; Biomechanical Analysis of Sport Performance—The Study of the Mechanics of Sport Motion Emphasizing Analysis of Sport Techniques and Exploration of Current Research and Instrumentation. For additional program information, write to the colleges of your choice; address your letter to the director of the exercise physiology program. The following schools offer such programs:

Arizona

Department of Physical Education
University of Arizona
Tucson, AZ 85721

California

Department of Physical Education
The University of California at Berkeley
Berkeley, CA 94720

Department of Exercise Physiology
The University of California at Davis
Davis, CA 95616

California State University at Fullerton
Department of Physical Education
Fullerton, CA 92634

Department of Physical Education
The University of Southern California
Los Angeles, CA 90024

Department of Physical Education
California State University at Sacramento
Sacramento, CA 95819

Connecticut

Department of Physical Education
University of Connecticut
Storrs, CT 06268

Florida

Department of Movement Science
Florida State University
Tallahassee, FL 32306

Georgia

Department of Health, Physical Education, Recreation and
Dance
Georgia State University
Atlanta, GA 30303

Indiana

Human Performance Laboratory
Ball State University
Muncie, IN 47306

Iowa

Department of Physical Education
University of Iowa
Iowa City, IA 52242

Illinois

Department of Education
Western Illinois University
Macomb, IL 61455

Kansas

Department of Health, Physical Education and Recreation
Kansas State University
Manhattan, KS 66506

Maryland

Department of Physical Education
University of Maryland
College Park, MD 20742

Massachusetts

Department of Exercise Science
University of Massachusetts
Amherst, MA 01003

Department of Health Sciences
Boston University
Boston, MA 02215

Department of Physical Education
Springfield College
Springfield, MA 01109

Michigan

Human Performance Laboratory
Central Michigan University
Mt. Pleasant, MI 48858

Missouri

Department of Health and Physical Education
University of Missouri
Columbia, MO 65201

New York

Department of Physical Education
Adelphi University
Garden City, NY 11530

Department of Physiology
SUNY Upstate Medical Center
Syracuse, NY 13210

North Carolina

Department of Physical Education
University of North Carolina
Chapel Hill, NC 27514

Bowman Gray School of Medicine
Wake Forest University
Winston-Salem, NC 27103

Ohio

Laboratory of Work Physiology
Ohio State University
Columbus, OH 43210

Applied Physiology Laboratory
Kent State University
Kent, OH 44242

Oklahoma

Department of Physiology and Biophysics
University of Oklahoma
Oklahoma City, OK 73190

Oregon

Department of Physical Education
University of Oregon
Eugene, OR 97403

Pennsylvania

College of Health, Physical Education and Recreation
The Pennsylvania State University
University Park, PA 16802

Texas

Department of Physical and Health Education
University of Texas
Austin, TX 78712

Department of Physical Education
Texas Christian University
Ft. Worth, TX 76129

Department of Health, Physical Education and Recreation
Texas Tech University
Lubbock, TX 79409

Virginia

Department of Health and Physical Education
University of Virginia
Charlottesville, VA 22903

Washington

Department of Kinesiology
University of Washington
Seattle, WA 98195

West Virginia

Medical Center
University of West Virginia
Morgantown, WV 26506

Wisconsin

School of Health and Physical Education
University of Wisconsin—La Crosse
La Crosse, WI 54601

School of Health, Physical Education and Recreation
University of Wisconsin
Madison, WI 53706

Wyoming

Department of Exercise Science
University of Wyoming
Laramie, WY 82070

AEROBICS INSTRUCTOR

The aerobics instructor at the health club is an important (but unfortunately not well-paying) career for those not wishing to take a rigorous academic program prior to entering a profession. The most common types of aerobic exercise in health clubs are stationary cycling, stair climbing, stationary rowing, walking, jogging, swimming, stationary cross country skiing, and aerobic dance.

Research indicates that when done properly, aerobic activity yields the following positive results:

- promotes strong and healthy bones
- helps control the physical and emotional stresses of life
- can improve intellectual capacity and increase productivity
- provides a realistic way to lose fat and keep it off
- provides significant protection from heart disease
- can achieve maximum benefits in a minimum amount of time

Those interested in this growing career of aerobic dance may wish to contact the NDEITA (National Dance Exercise Instructor's Training Association). This organization provides education, training, and certification to fitness professionals. They offer weekend workshops nationally to carry out the organization's goals. For information contact:

NDEITA
1503 South Washington Avenue
Minneapolis, MN 55454

The following organizations provide information and programs also:

The Association for Fitness in Business
310 N. Alabama, Suite A100
Indianapolis, IN 46204

National Women's Fitness Network
3518 Cahvengo Boulevard West
Suite 218
Los Angeles, CA 90068

The President's Council on Physical Fitness and Sports
Washington, DC 20001

Aerobic and Fitness Association of America
15250 Ventura Boulevard, Suite 802
Sherman Oaks, CA 91403

International Dance-Exercise Association
4501 Mission Bay Drive, Suite 2-F
San Diego, CA 92109

Jazzercise
2808 Roosevelt Street
Carlsbad, CA 92008

Aerobics Center
12200 Preston Road
Dallas, TX 75230

American Association of Fitness Directors in Business and
   Industry
400 6th Avenue S.W.
Washington, DC 20201

Dance Educators of America
Box 470
Caldwell, NJ 07006

American Dance Therapy Association
200 Century Plaza, Suite 108
Columbia, MD 21044

SPORTS MASSAGE THERAPY

The magic fingers of Bucky Grace (Penn Oaks Fitness and
Tennis Club, West Chester, Pennsylvania) are regularly found
assisting world-class runners. These individuals utilize the skills
of "Dr. Bucky" as part of their regular training program and in
pre-event preparation and postevent recovery. Neil Sherman (Chicago Health Club, Vernon Hills, Illinois) utilizes his "meat
hooks" (Chicago Bears football coach Mike Ditka's description)
to prepare coaches and players for competition.

Athletes have discovered the value of sports massage, and
massage therapists have expanded their practices to meet this
need.

The professional association of this career, the American Massage Therapy Association (AMTA), believes its practitioners can
offer significant benefits to athletes. Certification requires completion of an approved program from one of the approximately 55
institutions in the United States and Canada. Typical of such
schools is the sports massage curriculum at the Florida School of

Massage in Gainesville, Florida. Topics for students include scar tissue pathologies; creating a nurturing and supportive environment for the athlete; warm-up routines; and sports massage therapy for common athletic injuries. The program also features a supervised field experience.

While salaries vary widely ($18,000-$45,000 a year) the future looms very bright for this career. For additional information and a list of schools contact:

American Massage Therapy Association
1130 W. North Shore Avenue
Chicago, IL 60626

SPORTS ACUPUNCTURE AND RELATED THERAPIES

The current interest in complementary and alternative medical therapies has not escaped the sports community. Some athletes seek these nontraditional treatments for injuries, and an increasing number hope to achieve maximum performance through these means. Michael Ranft, C.A. (certified acupuncturist), explains the value of his therapy. ''Acupuncture is used to increase the flow of blood and energy enabling the athlete to perform better.'' Ranft, who holds a number of certificates in holistic medicine, maintains his office and practice in Hot Springs, Arkansas. He believes his orientation ''can make a difference in people's lives with no side effects. It's a wonderful complement to traditional medicine; in addition, we have a strong emphasis on prevention.'' Ranft utilizes acupuncture differently, depending on the athlete's sport. With runners, ''I direct the chi (energy flow) in the legs and lungs; naturally with a shot-putter I work differently.''

Colleges of acupuncture and oriental medicine function as most professional schools, requiring both course work and an internship. In addition, they offer short courses normally in the specialties of acupuncture, Chinese massage, and Chinese herbology. At the Florida Institute of Traditional Chinese Medicine, the complete program requires four-and-a-half years of study.

The following are typical of the courses offered at the American College of Traditional Chinese Medicine in San Francisco.

- Nutrition and the Treatment of Disease: General concepts of nutrition as a treatment modality in traditional Chinese medicine. Differential diagnosis and symptom/sign complex is reviewed for nutritional treatment of various diseases with presentation of appropriate use of diet, herbal stews, and soup.
- Diseases of Women as Treated by Traditional Chinese Medicine: Diagnosis and treatment of abnormal menstruation, pregnancy complications, sterility, fibroid tumors, and herpes. Case studies are presented.

A number of colleges exist to serve interested students wishing to pursue this aspect of medicine and use it in sports. Interested individuals should contact:

American Association of Acupuncture and Oriental Medicine
1424 16th Street N.W., Suite 501
Washington, DC 20036

Those interested in alternative medical approaches will find two resources of particular interest: *East/West: The Journal of Natural Health and Living,* P.O. Box 52372, Boulder, CO 80321-2372; and *Homeopathy: Medicine for the 21st Century,* North Atlantic Books, 1988.

SPORTS PSYCHOLOGISTS

Joan Ingalls emphasizes "visual training and mental practices skills" in her career as a sports psychologist. An adjunct faculty member at William Patterson College in Wayne, New Jersey, she maintains a private practice in New York City. She believes her psychological techniques lead to "performance enhancement by athletes." She also believes (as do most sports psychologists), "I can work with 'troubled' athletes, but I like to think of myself as an educator rather than a therapist." With a background in rowing and tennis competition and collegiate work at Ohio State, Goddard College, and Columbia University, Ingalls typifies many of today's sports psychologists who successfully assist athletes.

Research studies of psychological needs and behaviors of athletes have been conducted by psychologists for many years. However, only since the 1960s has a concerted study focused on the general psychological aspects of sports and the psychological behaviors of athletes.

Sports psychologists engage essentially in two activities. One group serves as faculty at institutions of higher education with teaching as their major function. Part of their duties involve research, which they devote to topics related to sport psychology. They investigate areas such as the ones discussed in the following articles that appeared in a recent issue of *The Journal of Sport Psychology: "Immediate Effects of Win-Loss on Perceptions of Cohesion in Intramural and Intercollegiate Volleyball Teams"; "The Influence of Socializing Agents on Female Collegiate Volleyball Players"; "Intraindividual Pregame State Anxiety and Basketball Performance: A Re-examination of the Inverted-U-Curve"; "The Influence of Level of Sports Participation and Sex-role Orientation on Female Professionalization of Attitudes toward Play."*

Some sports psychologists have a private practice or group practice. These individuals see athletes with problems on an individual basis and work with teams. The Sports Psychology Institute located in Roslyn Heights, Long Island, New York, is typical. The institute states its purpose as "designed to enhance competitive athletic performance through self-regulative training and specially devised individual programs in sports hypno-imagery." Some sports psychologists work with professional athletes suffering from alcohol or drug abuse.

Dr. George Pollock, a psychiatrist and director of the Chicago Institute for Psychoanalysis, has successfully worked with many professional athletes with personal problems.

A few college instructors maintain a part-time professional office practice or serve as consultants to teams. Dr. Richard M. Suinn, department head of psychology, Colorado State University, works with relaxation and visualization techniques in aiding athletes. He utilizes these methods to combat the negative thinking of some athletes. Among his strategies, Dr. Suinn has the athlete mentally visualize past successful experiences, thereby increasing his or her self-confidence.

Another topic of recent interest to the general sports community that also interests sports psychologists is burnout. Bill Beavsay, Ph.D., executive director of the Academy for the Psychology of Sports, feels stress lies at the basis of the problem experienced by many players and coaches. There exists some general agreement among sports psychologists that the solution lies in rest and diversion—athletes and coaches must have interests other than sports.

One cautious note about this profession is sounded by William Morgan, Ph.D., director of the sports psychology laboratory at the University of Wisconsin and consultant to several teams. Dr. Morgan believes a crisis exists in the field of sports psychology because only about "five percent of all sport psychologists have been actually trained in sport *and* psychology.'' This means that many individuals with backgrounds in physical education, kinesiology, human kinetics, and sports studies are working as sports psychologists without proper credentials. This also means that many opportunities will exist for persons, properly trained, who wish to enter the field.

Education

Sports psychology normally requires a doctorate, although some may be able to practice privately with a master's degree. Texas Christian University offers a master of science program in which the student can take sports psychology. Psychological Dimensions of Sport and Play, Social Psychology of Play Based Activity, and Seminar in Kinesiological Psychology are some courses that would be taken in such a program. Doctoral studies normally require four or five years of study beyond the completion of college. Those who might be interested should pursue advanced course work in psychology (if available) and mathematics (statistics is important in psychology) at the high school level. Majoring in psychology along with some electives in sport studies should form the emphasis of the undergraduate program. The courses at the doctoral level will feature advanced studies in physiology, human behavior, personality theories, statistics, and motivation. It will be important to locate a Ph.D. program that emphasizes people and will permit some elective course work in human performance science and sport studies. Naturally, good to excellent grades will be important throughout school.

The expanding role of the sports psychologist means that future members of this young profession will help to shape it. Many professional teams have psychologists as consultants, and the field is not limited to men—Julie Anthony, Ph.D., assisted the Philadelphia Flyers (she now serves as director of the Aspen Fitness and Sports Medicine Institute), and college teams have begun to move in this direction; perhaps you will be serving in this capacity in a few short years. For additional information consult: *The Journal of Sports Psychology,* published by Human Kinetics Publishers, Box 5076, Champaign, IL 61820. You may also want to read a classic book, *The Miracle of Sports Psychology: How to Win with Mental Dynamics,* Englewood Cliffs, New Jersey, Prentice-Hall. Also, you may wish to contact the Academy for the Psychology of Sports, 2062 Arlington Avenue, Toledo, OH 43609. A pamphlet entitled *Sport Psychology and Counseling* is available from Sports Psychology Program, University of North Carolina at Greensboro, Greensboro, NC 27412.

CHAPTER 6

SPORTS MEDICINE PARAPROFESSIONALS

Numerous paraprofessionals assist in a variety of capacities in the sports medicine profession. The term *paraprofessional* refers to health people who assist professionals (such as doctors and physical therapists) in the performance of their duties. Recently, these aides, with advanced training, have been permitted to undertake many of the duties previously done by professionals.

The characteristics of paraprofessionals include:

- Serving under the supervision of a professional. The amount of responsibility given to the paraprofessional varies with experience and training. For example, a physical therapy assistant may provide rehabilitation instructions to an injured high school basketball player with a sprained ankle.
- Usually, completing an education/training program, normally at a college. Some persons with experience may have shorter field programs. For example, most podiatric assistants receive on-the-job training. However, to become certified, the individual must pass an examination prepared by the American Society of Podiatric Assistants. On the other hand, most states require a two-year college training program followed by a state exam for licensing as physical therapy assistant.

- The nature of the paraprofessional's education/training resembles that of the profession to which it corresponds, except that it is shorter and more limited in content. For example, the physical therapy assistant program includes curriculum courses such as anatomy, physiology, psychology, physical therapy procedures, and philosophy of rehabilitation.

Paraprofessionals now work in many sports medicine fields. This offers the individual with an interest in sports medicine the opportunity for an enjoyable and rewarding career.

GENERAL SPORTS MEDICINE AIDES

A number of sports medicine professionals and clinics employ individuals as aides. These people, who learn their duties on the job, assist both professionals and paraprofessionals. Many become very interested in their career and will seek schooling to improve themselves and their salaries. If you are interested in these occupations, apply directly to the private offices of sports medicine professionals or to centers that specialize in sports medicine. Often these jobs provide excellent insight into the world of sports and make good summer positions. Some colleges offer two-year programs to train medical assistants. In addition, some proprietary schools offer medical secretarial curricula. Future job opportunities will continue to increase.

SPORTS PODIATRIC ASSISTANT

Podiatric assistants aid podiatrists in performing functions related to the medical health of the sport participant's lower extremities. They perform functions such as recording patient histories, preparing instruments and equipment, applying surgical dressings, preparing patients for treatment, and assisting with routine office procedures.

While many programs are developing to educate podiatric assistants, most receive on-the-job training. Many qualify for the designation P.A.C. (podiatric assistant certified) from the American Society of Podiatric Associates; eligibility for certification requires membership in the society and the passing of an exam prepared by it. Normally, certification carries with it improved prestige and increased salary. For additional information contact:

American Society of Podiatric Assistants
2204 Washington Avenue
Waco, TX 76702

SPORTS PHYSICAL THERAPY ASSISTANT

Physical therapy assistants work under the supervision of a physical therapist. In this capacity they help injured athletes, usually at a sports clinic, through rehabilitation.

Because the sports physical therapy assistant job is more advanced in its development than the other sports medical paraprofessional careers, most states require a two-year training program followed by a written exam prepared by the board of medical examiners of the state. Successful completion grants the candidate a license as a physical therapy assistant.

Some of the major duties of the sports physical therapist include:

- Assisting the injured athlete through a wide range of treatments prescribed by doctors and therapists
- Reporting the progress of the injured athlete undergoing a variety of therapeutic techniques to the physical therapist

- Giving exercise instructions to the rehabilitated player to avoid future injuries
- Providing guidance in using an orthopedic device if utilized in maximizing the athlete's performance and diminishing the possibility of another injury
- Offering support and empathy to the injured athlete
- Instructing and giving directions to physical therapy aides

Typical of the educational programs available is the physical therapy assistant program at Harcum Junior College in Bryn Mawr, Pennsylvania. Students at Harcum pursue a two-year program undertaking courses in Applied Kinesiology, Human Anatomy and Physiology, Rehabilitation, and Physical Therapy in addition to regular college courses. During the second semester of the second year, the program culminates in a sixteen-credit clinical practicum. At this time, the student with an interest in sports athletics indicates a desire to work in the office of a sports physical therapist or at a sports medicine clinic or center. During the practicum, the student, under the supervision of a college supervisor and a physical therapist at the site, obtains valuable practical experience in two different settings.

Presently, most physical therapy assistants who assist injured athletes work with physical therapists in their offices or at sports medicine centers or clinics. Research indicates future job opportunities will become available at sports medicine centers. Here, therapy assistants will serve as part of a team evaluating, diagnosing, rehabilitating, and preventing injuries. Salaries (beginning from $18,000–$21,000) and job opportunities are presently good and will improve throughout the decade of the 1990s. As sports medicine expands, so will the need for physical therapy assistants. A list of approved colleges follows:

Alabama

University of Alabama in Birmingham
Physical Therapist Assistant Program, Division of Physical Therapy
School of Community and Allied Health
RTI Building, Room B41
Birmingham, AL 35294

California

DeAnza Community College
Physical Therapist Assistant Program
21250 Stevens Creek Boulevard
Cupertino, CA 95014

Mount St. Mary's College
Physical Therapist Assistant Program
10 Chester Place
Los Angeles, CA 90049

Cerritos College
Physical Therapist Assistant Program, Health Occupations Division
11110E Allondra Boulevard
Norwalk, CA 90650

San Diego Mesa College
Physical Therapist Assistant Program
7250 Mesa College Drive
San Diego, CA 92111

Los Angeles Pierce College
Physical Therapist Assistant Program
6201 Winnetka Avenue
Woodland Hills, CA 91371

Florida

Broward Community College
Physical Therapist Assistant Program, Division of Allied Health
3501 S.W. Davie Road
Ft. Lauderdale, FL 33314

Miami-Dade Community College
Physical Therapist Assistant Program
Medical Center Campus
950 N.W. 20th Street
Miami, FL 33127

St. Petersburg Junior College
Physical Therapist Assistant Program
P.O. Box 13498
St. Petersburg, FL 33733

Georgia

Medical College of Georgia
Physical Therapist Assistant Program
School of Allied Health Sciences
1120 15th Street
Augusta, GA 30912

Illinois

Belleville Area College
Physical Therapist Assistant Program
2500 Carlyle Road
Belleville, IL 62221

Southern Illinois University
Physical Therapist Program, School of Technical Careers
Wham 141
Carbondale, IL 62901

Morton College
Physical Therapist Assistant Program
3801 S. Central Avenue
Cicero, IL 69650

Oakton Community College
Physical Therapist Assistant Program
1600 E. Golf Road, Cluster 2
Des Plaines, IL 60016

Illinois Central College
Physical Therapist Assistant Program
East Peoria, IL 61635

Indiana

University of Evansville
Physical Therapist Assistant Program
P.O. Box 320
Evansville, IN 47714

Vincennes University
Physical Therapist Assistant Program, Health Occupations
   Department
1002 N. 1st Street
Vincennes, IN 47591

Kansas

Colby Community College
Physical Therapist Assistant Program
1255 South Range
Colby, KS 67701

Kentucky

Jefferson Community College
Physical Therapist Assistant Program, Division of Allied Health
P.O.B. 1036
Louisville, KY 40201

Maryland

Community College of Baltimore
Physical Therapist Assistant Program
3901 Liberty Heights Avenue
Baltimore, MD 21215

Massachusetts

North Shore Community College
Physical Therapist Program
3 Essex Street
Beverly, MA 01915

Newbury Junior College
Physical Therapist Assistant Program
100 Summer Street
Holliston, MA 01746

Lasell Junior College
Physical Therapist Assistant Program
Newton, MA 02166

Springfield Technical Community College
Physical Therapist Assistant Program
One Armory Square
Springfield, MA 01105

Becker Junior College
Physical Therapists Assistant Program, Health and Social Services
    Department
61 Sever Street
Worcester, MA 01609

Michigan

Kellogg Community College
Physical Therapist Assistant Program
450 North Avenue
Battle Creek, MI 49016

Delta College
Physical Therapist Assistant Program
F-53 Allied Health Building
University Center, MI 48710

Minnesota

St. Mary's Junior College
Physical Therapist Assistant Program
2500 S. Sixth Street
Minneapolis, MN 55454

Missouri

Penn Valley Community College
Physical Therapist Program
3201 Southwest Trafficway
Kansas City, MO 64111

New Hampshire

New Hampshire Vocational-Technical College
Physical Therapist Assistant Program
Hanover Street, Extension
Claremont, NH 03743

New Jersey

Union County College
Physical Therapist Assistant Program
1033 Springfield Avenue
Cranford, NJ 07016

Fairleigh-Dickinson University
Physical Therapist Assistant Program
Florham-Madison Campus
285 Madison Avenue
Madison, NJ 07940

Atlantic Community College
Physical Therapist Assistant Program
Allied Health Division
Mays Landing, NJ 08330

Essex County College
Physical Therapist Program
303 University Avenue
Newark, NJ 07102

New York

Maria College
Physical Therapist Assistant Program
700 New Scotland
Albany, NY 12208-1798

Nassau Community College
Physical Therapist Assistant Program
Stewart Avenue
Garden City, NY 11530

Orange County Community College
Physical Therapist Assistant Program
115 South Street
Middletown, NY 10940

Institute of Rehabilitation Medicine
Physical Therapist Assistant Program
New York University Medical Center
400 E. 34th Street
New York, NY 10016

Suffolk County Community College
Physical Therapist Assistant Program
533 College Road
Selden, NY 11784

North Carolina

Central Piedmont Community College
Physical Therapist Assistant Program
P.O.B. 35009
Charlotte, NC 28235

Fayetteville Technical Institute
Physical Therapist Assistant Program
P.O.B. #35236
Fayetteville, NC 28303

Ohio

Stark Technical College
Physical Therapist Assistant Program, Allied Health Technologies
6200 Frank Avenue NW
Canton, OH 44720

Cuyahoga Community College
Physical Therapist Assistant Program
Metropolitan Campus
2900 Community College Avenue
Cleveland, OH 44115

Sinclair Community College
Physical Therapist Assistant Program
444 W. Third Street
Dayton, OH 45402

Oregon

Mount Hood Community College
Physical Therapist Assistant Program, Allied Health Department of
    Physical Therapy
26000 S.E. Stark
Gresham, OR 97030

Pennsylvania

Harcum Junior College
Physical Therapist Assistant Program
Bryn Mawr, PA 19010

Pennsylvania State University
Physical Therapist Assistant Program
Box 710A
Hazleton, PA 18201

Lehigh County Community College
Physical Therapist Assistant Program
2370 Main Street
Schnecksville, PA 18078

Puerto Rico

The University of Puerto Rico, Humacao University College
Physical Therapist Assistant Program
CUH Station
Humacao, PR 00661

Ponce Regional College/The University of Puerto Rico
Physical Therapist Assistant Program
P.O. Box 7186
Ponce, PR 00732

South Carolina

Greenville Technical Collge
Physical Therapist Assistant Program
Box 5616, Station B
Greenville, SC 29606

Tennessee

Chattanooga State Technical Community College
Physical Therapist Assistant Program, Division of Life and Health
    Sciences
4501 Amnicola Highway
Chattanooga, TN 37406

Shelby State Community College
Physical Therapist Assistant Program, Division of Allied Health
P.O. Box 40568
Memphis, TN 48174-0578

Volunteer State Community College
Physical Therapist Assistant Program, Allied Health P-205
Nashville Pike
Gallatin, TN 37066

Texas

Houston Community College
Physical Therapist Assistant Program
3200 Shenandoah
Houston, TX 77021

Tarrant County Junior College
Physical Therapist Assistant Program
Northeast Campus
828 Harwood Road
Hurst, TX 76053

St. Philip's Community College
Physical Therapist Assistant Program
2111 Nevada Street
San Antonio, TX 78203

Virginia

Northern Virginia Community College
Physical Therapist Assistant Program
8333 Little River Turnpike
Annandale, VA 22003

Washington

Green River Community College
Physical Therapist Assistant Program
12401 SE 320th Street
Auburn, WA 98002

Wisconsin

Milwaukee Area Technical College
Physical Therapist Assistant Program, Health Occupations Division
1015 N. 6th Street
Milwaukee, WI 53203

U.S. Air Force Medical Department

Community College of the Air Force
Physical Therapist Assistant Program
Group Intermediate Supervisor 913XO Courses
School of Health Care Sciences, MSDB, Stop 114
Sheppard Air Force Base, TX 76311

SPORTS VISION PARAPROFESSIONALS

A number of paraprofessionals assist doctors in the care of vision.

Ophthalmologists, medical doctors (M.D.), have assistants as do optometrists (O.D.). The development of these paraprofessional careers has made a major impact on eye care professionals.

Sports Ophthalmic Assistant and Technician

Ophthalmic assistants and technicians perform a variety of functions related to eye care, for example:

- obtain an ophthalmic history of an athlete including present problems
- perform certain measurements of the eye
- maintain instruments

More advanced assistants perform more sophisticated procedures. Likewise, the ophthalmic technician, whose training exceeds that of assistants, can engage in more technical procedures. These would include assisting the ophthalmologist in eye surgery.

The joint commission on Allied Health Personnel in Ophthalmology serves as the governing board for paraprofessionals in this area. As such, it approves training programs and conducts national certification examinations for assistants and technicians. While certification is not required for employment, it assists in obtaining a position and will contribute to improved salary.

Income for experienced ophthalmic assistants averages approximately $25,000 a year, and salaries for ophthalmic technicians range from $23,000 to $40,000. Job opportunities continue to look excellent as additional athletes recognize the importance of vision to their performance. To obtain additional information contact:

Joint Commission on Allied Health
Personnel in Ophthalmology
1812 N. St. Paul Road
St. Paul, MN 55109

Sports Optometric Assistant and Technician

Sports optometric assistants and technicians assist eye care professionals in a variety of ways. They normally serve in the private office or clinic of an optometrist (O.D.) who specializes in sports vision. Working with athletes, they:

- undertake preliminary tests of vision
- assist in implementation of a vision improvement program
- record data as the doctor measures sports vision improvement
- provide assistance with appointments, billing, and record keeping

Some formal programs now exist to train assistants; optometrists favor hiring these trained individuals. However, most assistants receive on-the-job training. The technician must complete a more extensive course of study. The program, lasting two years, focuses upon courses in anatomy, physiology of the human eye, office procedures, and related courses. Upon graduation, the candidate is awarded an associate degree in optometric technicianry. While not required for employment, registration is possible. To qualify, the candidate must have the proper education, experience, and successful completion of an examination. The American Optometric Association National Para-Optometric Registry serves to list the candidate as a registered optometric assistant or registered optometric technician.

The general employment outlook is good in the field of eye care. Likewise, growing interest in sports vision makes prospects very good in the 1990s. Earnings, which average $18,000 for assistants and $21,000 for technicians, vary with training and experience. For further information contact:

The American Optometric Association
243 N. Lindbergh Boulevard
St. Louis, MO 63141

ORTHOTIC/PROSTHETIC ASSISTANT AND TECHNICIAN

These paraprofessionals assist the orthotist and/or prosthetist in providing care to injured athletes. Specifically, the assistant, who may have taken some courses in orthotics or prosthetics but probably obtained most of his or her training on the job, works closely with the professional orthotist/prosthetist. Together they carry out the directions given by the medical doctor—usually an orthopedist. Often the orthotist assistant will make sure the injured athlete is properly utilizing the orthotic device and if a problem exists, will report it to the orthotist. Frequently, the assistant will take additional course work and eventually qualify for and pass the appropriate exam to become an orthotist/prosthetist.

Likewise, the orthotic technician supports the orthotist in providing care to athletes by fabricating devices, known as orthoses. The technician repairs these devices and keeps abreast of new developments in materials.

The prosthetic technician assists the prosthetist to aid the athlete who has partial or total loss of a limb by constructing a device known as a prosthesis. The technician must maintain familiarity with materials and techniques so as to provide the finest quality possible.

Technicians may obtain certification through the American Board of Certification in Orthotics and Prosthetics. In addition to meeting educational and experience criteria, they must pass an examination. Successful completion of these steps carries with it the title registered technician (orthotics) [R.T.O.] or registered technician prosthetics [R.T.P.] or registered technician (orthotics-prosthetics) [R.T.(O.P.)].

These paraprofessionals earn a good but not exceptional livelihood, which may be improved by moving up in the field. The satisfaction of assisting an injured athlete in returning to competition serves as a major reward for these individuals.

For additional information, contact:

The American Board for Certification in Orthotics and
   Prosthetics
717 Pendleton Street
Alexandria, VA 22314

SPORTS DENTAL PARAPROFESSIONALS

The growing realization of the importance of dental fitness by athletes coupled with a strong interest by some dentists in sports medicine opens opportunities for paraprofessionals interested in sports dentistry. Three categories of paraprofessions exist in this area: the dental hygienist, the dental assistant, and the dental technician.

The Dental Hygienist

The dental hygienist serves as an oral health clinician and educator who promotes dental fitness through oral health and preventive dentistry. The duties of the dental hygienist vary widely but generally include the following:

- Recording medical and dental histories

- Providing the patient with information concerning dental health practices
- Removing deposits and stains from teeth
- Assisting the dentist with x-rays
- Aiding the patient with pain control

Dental hygienists attend college—most receive their associate degree from a two-year collge while a few obtain a bachelor's and master's degree. It should be noted that some schools require applicants to take the Dental Hygiene Aptitude Test prior to admission. Following graduation, the hygienist must be licensed by the state; this means successfully passing a written and clinical examination.

Salaries for dental hygienists are moderately good with opportunities for improved income with additional education. Additional information and a list of accredited schools may be obtained from the following organization:

American Dental Hygienists Association
444 N. Michigan Avenue
Chicago, IL 60611

The Dental Assistant

Dental assistants aid the dentist in providing care to patients. They typically engage in the following activities:

- Seating the patient in the dental chair and preparing him or her for treatment
- Giving the dentist the patient's record and setting the tray with the appropriate materials
- Handing the dentist the necessary instruments and materials for keeping the patient's mouth clear
- Preparing materials for dental impressions and developing x-rays

- Performing routine office procedures such as patient billing and ordering dental supplies

Community colleges and technical schools offer programs for dental assistants. Typical of these programs is the one offered at the College of Lake County in Grayslake, Illinois. The dental assistant program leading to a certificate requires a commitment of two regular semesters and a summer. Students enroll in courses such as Dental Science I; Professionalism and Ethics; and Radiology. One required course, Dental Office Practice, has the following description: "Introduction to general office routine, charting, insurance, records, files, financial statements and written communications necessary to the smooth operation of the dental office." The practically oriented program requires 39 credits for completion. Graduates of accredited programs may take a national certification exam. Certified dental assistants obtain better salaries (beginning at approximately $18,000–$20,000 a year) and positions; it would be difficult to obtain a position without certification. For additional information contact:

American Dental Assistants Association
680 N. Lake Shore Drive
Chicago, IL 60611

Certifying Board of the ADAA
680 N. Lake Shore Drive
Chicago, IL 60611

The Dental Technician

Dental technicians work in dental laboratories where they construct a variety of dental appliances. However, sports dentistry clinics frequently have labs associated with them which serve as employment possibilities. Education takes two forms—apprenticeship programs conducted by commercial laboratories or two-year programs in dental technology, usually at a technical school or community college.

Beginning technicians' salaries rank below that of their fellow paraprofessionals; however, with experience, their income grows quickly. The growth of the use of mouth pieces for safety and to improve performance will make dental laboratory technical work an enjoyable and interesting specialty in the future. For additional information contact:

American Dental Association
211 E. Chicago Avenue
Chicago, IL 60611

National Association of Dental Laboratories
3801 Mount Vernon Avenue
Alexandria, VA 22305

For information about dental paraprofessional careers, consult VGM Career Horizon's *Opportunities in Dental Care Careers.* You may also wish to consult the VGM Career Horizons book *Opportunities in Paramedical Careers.*

For the individual with an interest in sports, these paraprofessional careers offer excellent opportunities. An interest and knowledge of the sciences remain an important prerequisite for entry into these jobs. An additional financial consideration concerns the fact that more often individuals employed in sports centers or in the office of a sports medical specialist receive salaries above those in more traditional settings.

The expanding world of sports careers offers something for everyone. For those not wishing a lengthy collegiate education, careers as sports paraprofessionals offer a viable alternative and are clearly worthy of investigation by those interested in jobs in sports and athletics.

CHAPTER 7

GETTING STARTED

A few years ago high school freshman Brad Curley earned a varsity letter for football on the state championship team at Holliston (Massachusetts) High School. Brad weighed ninety pounds and stood five feet tall!

You guessed it, Brad was the varsity football team's student athletic trainer. An excellent way to gain knowledge concerning sports medicine careers is to serve as a student athletic trainer for a high school or college athletic team. With the rapid growth of a number of minor sports (soccer, track, lacrosse) and the increased participation in women's sports, many schools at all levels beg for athletic training help. Student athletic trainers normally engage in the following activities:

- Assist in maintaining the training room and the supplies
- Aid with taping and treatments
- Prepare field kits and have them available during contests and practice
- Report new injuries to coach and trainer
- Prepare beverages and have them ready for breaks during games and practice
- Complete a course for student trainers

- Keep student athletic trainer duties separate from student manager responsibilities
- Help in record keeping of player injuries and treatment
- Perform related tasks as requested by the coach, trainer, or physician
- Maintain a professional rapport with players, coaches, physician, trainer, and with the opposing team and its personnel

Since 1957, Cramer Products, which produces and sells a broad range of athletic equipment, training room supplies, and first aid products, has conducted student athletic trainer workshops. The sessions, designed for junior high and high school students, teach the fundamentals of athletic injury care and prevention. In addition, many sports medicine centers and universities and colleges independently sponsor clinics and workshops for student athletic trainers. The Cramer Athletic Training Workshop, conducted over a period of three days (including evenings), covers topics such as the following: basic physiology of treatment, wound management, head and neck injuries, heat problems, facial injuries, transporting injured athletes, and knee injuries. The students not only hear lectures and observe demonstrations but engage in hands-on activities developing knowledge, skill and practice.

One of the lectures given relates to the fundamentals of taping and wrapping. The following outline details the depth of the instruction.

Fundamentals of Taping and Wrapping

A. Basic taping theory
  1. Functions of tape (controlling–stabilizing range of motion)
     a. Prevention
     b. Support
     c. Protection

2. Selection of tape
    a. Grades of tape
    b. Width of tape
    c. Care and storage of tape
    d. Budget consideration
3. Position of athlete/body part when taping
4. Position of trainer when taping
    a. Body mechanics
    b. Height of table or taping surface

B. Tearing and handling of tape
C. Preparation of area to be taped
    1. Cleanliness
    2. Shaved
    3. Normal body temperature
    4. Use of adherents
    5. Use of lubricants—pads on Achilles area, instep, and back of knee
    6. Use of underwrap
    7. Possibility of skin irritations

D. Taping
    1. Anchors—directly to skin vs. over underwrap
    2. Stirrup
    3. Angulation
    4. Amount of pressure on application
    5. Overlapping
    6. Wrinkles—neatness
    7. Durability—will the tape job hold up?
    8. Pride in work

E. Removal of tape
    1. Tape cutters, scissors—use of lubricant on implement to reduce friction
    2. Prudence in removal of tape
    3. Clean skin of tape residue

    F. The ankle wrap
        1. When used and why
        2. Material and length
    G. The elastic wrap
        1. When used and why
        2. Material, width, and length
        3. Care
            a. Economics
            b. Launder and reuse

Coaches are clearly convinced of the value of a well-prepared student athletic trainer. Football coach Dewey Schiele of Waukesha, Wisconsin, North High School had the good fortune of utilizing Mark Sinotte, a premed student at Marquette University, for three years as an athletic trainer. Mark not only assisted the players but helped initiate a student trainer program. Coach Schiele echoes the sentiments of many coaches when he states, "They'd [the athletic coaches] rather see some person specifically trained in athletic injuries around, which leaves more coaching responsibility to themselves."

Jim Routier, A.T.C., athletic trainer at Concord High School, has developed an excellent program for student trainers. Normally he has a number of young people wishing to serve as trainers. He carefully selects those individuals who have a history of reliability, enjoy athletics, and get along well with people. Those chosen are made to feel part of the athletic program and the team for which they work. Jim Routier has set up a fine reward system for those in his program.

Student Trainer Award Program

CONCORD HIGH SCHOOL, ELKHART, INDIANA

FIRST LEVEL (NOVICE)

1. Application accepted
2. Three weeks observation
3. 250 hours of work time in training room
4. Completion of Cramer Student Trainer Course

AWARD: Varsity letter and chevron
SECOND LEVEL (STUDENT TRAINER)

1. 500 hours of work time in training room
2. Completion of workshop or equivalent
3. Completion of practical test on skills and knowledge

AWARD: 2-year chevron and pin
THIRD LEVEL (ADVANCED)

1. 750 total hours of work time in training room
2. CPR certification
3. Completion of Cramer Workshop or equivalent
4. Completion of practical test on skills and knowledge

AWARD: 3-year chevron and advanced student trainer pin
FOURTH LEVEL (MASTER)

1. 1,000 total hours of work time in training room
2. Master student training test on skills and knowledge
3. Responsibility for one complete seasonal sport

AWARD: Plaque and master pin
PROFESSIONAL LEVEL

1. 1,500 total hours of work time in training room
2. Professional practical test on skills and knowledge

AWARD: Receive plaque; name goes on professional honor plaque

It is hoped that programs like this will undergo adoption by many school districts.

Aspiring student athletic trainers are strongly encouraged to participate in a Cramer Workshop. Often schools will pay for expenses, travel, and the registration fee. Offered during the summers at many geographically well dispersed colleges, a list of recent locations follows:

Samford University
    Birmingham, AL
Arizona State University
    Tempe, AZ
Florida State University
    Tallahassee, FL
University of Idaho
    Moscow, ID
Northern Illinois University
    DeKalb, IL
Eastern Kentucky University
    Richmond, KY
Emporia State University
    Emporia, KS
Louisiana State University
    Baton Rouge, LA
North Adams State College
    North Adams, MA
Grand Valley State College
    Allendale, MI
Gustavus Adolphus College
    St. Peter, MN

Fresno State University
    Fresno, CA
University of Southern Colorado
    Pueblo, CO
Maryville—St. Louis
    Creve Coeur, MO
Kent State University
    Kent, OH
Oklahoma State University
    Stillwater, OK
Bloomsburg State College
    Bloomsburg, PA
Clemson University
    Clemson, SC
Memphis State University
    Memphis, TN
University of Texas—Arlington
    Arlington, TX
University of Virginia
    Charlottesville, VA
Seattle Pacific University
    Seattle, WA

SPORTS MEDICINE BIBLIOGRAPHY

A growing list of books on sports medicine is becoming available to the public. Those aspiring to enter sports medicine careers can become more familiar with the profession by reading the books listed below.

The Asthmatic Athlete—A short book that discusses the problem of exercise-induced asthma, methods of exercise testing, and patient management of the asthmatic athlete. American Medical Association.

Comments in Sports Medicine—A review of sports medicine issues including athletic injuries, athletic accident prevention, equipment and supplies, nutrition, and physical fitness. American Medical Association.

The Diabetic Athlete—Describes diabetes and hypoglycemia (two health problems related to the human body's use of sugar) and the value of exercise in this regard. American Medical Association.

First-Aid Chart for Athletic Injuries—Prepared by the Committee on the Medical Aspects of Sports, this wall chart includes recommendations about emergency care of the injured athlete. American Medical Association.

Fundamentals of Athletic Training—Outlines the duties and functions of the athletic trainer. This well-written book includes information on basic fitness practices, physical conditioning, and first aid. American Medical Association.

Medical Evaluation of the Athlete: A Guide—Discusses guidelines for the medical evaluation of athletes and includes disqualifying physical conditions for sports participation; prepared by the Committee on the Medical Aspects of Sports. American Medical Association.

Sports and Physical Fitness—Journal of the American Medical Association Questions and Answers. A short booklet provides answers to commonly asked questions on the topic. American Medical Association.

Sports Injuries—An Aid to Prevention and Treatment—An excellent book that provides practical illustrated suggestions on the topics of physical fitness, minimizing sports injuries treatment, and rehabilitation of sports injuries. Write Public Relations Department, Bufferin, P.O. Box 537, Coventry, CT 06238.

Sports Injury Care—A fine short booklet that carefully details many injuries, providing suggested treatment and how to prevent reoccurrence; recommends products to aid in both. Cramer Products, P.O. Box 1001, Gardner, KS 66030.

The AMA books and booklets may be obtained from:

Publications: Order Department
American Medical Association
P.O. Box 10946
Chicago, IL 60610

Three somewhat technical magazines exist that can provide a view of the nature of, and issues and developments in sports medicine.

The American Journal of Sports Medicine
428 E. Preston Street
Baltimore, MD 21202

Medicine and Science in Sports and Exercise
(Official Journal of the American College of Sports Medicine)
1 Virginia Avenue, Suite 340
Indianapolis, IN 46206

The Physician and Sports Medicine
McGraw-Hill Offices
4530 W. 77th Street
Minneapolis, MN 55435

These publications may be too expensive to purchase a subscription until you enter the profession; however, you can read them at most major public and university libraries. A valuable newsletter, *The First Aider,* is a fine publication that regularly covers sports medicine problems of concern to coaches and sports medicine specialists. The address to write is:

The First Aider
Cramer Products
P.O. Box 1001
Gardner, KS 66030

Also strongly recommended is membership in the National Athletic Trainers Association as a student member; the address follows:

National Athletic Trainers Association
2952 Stemmons Freeway
Suite 200
Dallas, TX 75247-6103

Volunteering and serving as a student athletic trainer opens the door to the world of sports medicine. It moves the volunteer close to the action to observe the many medical and allied medical specialists associated with the world of sports and athletics performing their tasks.

More importantly, it helps answer questions such as "What does an athletic trainer do the day of a game or contest?" "Should I consider becoming a sports medical doctor?" "How does a sports physician help players with foot problems?"

Not every profession has the type of opportunity that sports medicine presents for those considering joining it. It is strongly suggested that those considering sports medicine careers avail themselves of the awareness, orientation, knowledge, and skill development that the job of student athletic trainer offers.

VGM CAREER BOOKS

OPPORTUNITIES IN
Available in both paperback and hardbound editions

Accounting Careers
Acting Careers
Advertising Careers
Aerospace Careers
Agriculture Careers
Airline Careers
Animal and Pet Care
Appraising Valuation Science
Architecture
Automotive Service
Banking
Beauty Culture
Biological Sciences
Biotechnology Careers
Book Publishing Careers
Broadcasting Careers
Building Construction Trades
Business Communication Careers
Business Management
Cable Television
Carpentry Careers
Chemical Engineering
Chemistry Careers
Child Care Careers
Chiropractic Health Care
Civil Engineering Careers
Commercial Art and Graphic Design
Computer Aided Design and Computer Aided Mfg.
Computer Maintenance Careers
Computer Science Careers
Counseling & Development
Crafts Careers
Culinary Careers
Dance
Data Processing Careers
Dental Care
Drafting Careers
Electrical Trades
Electronic and Electrical Engineering
Electronics Careers
Energy Careers
Engineering Careers
Engineering Technology Careers
Environmental Careers
Eye Care Careers
Fashion Careers
Fast Food Careers
Federal Government Careers
Film Careers
Financial Careers
Fire Protection Services
Fitness Careers
Food Services
Foreign Language Careers
Forestry Careers
Gerontology Careers
Government Service
Graphic Communications
Health and Medical Careers
High Tech Careers
Home Economics Careers
Hospital Administration
Hotel & Motel Management
Human Resources Management Careers
Information Systems Careers

Insurance Careers
Interior Design
International Business
Journalism Careers
Landscape Architecture
Laser Technology
Law Careers
Law Enforcement and Criminal Justice
Library and Information Science
Machine Trades
Magazine Publishing Careers
Management
Marine & Maritime Careers
Marketing Careers
Materials Science
Mechanical Engineering
Medical Technology Careers
Metalworking Careers
Microelectronics
Military Careers
Modeling Careers
Music Careers
Newspaper Publishing Careers
Nursing Careers
Nutrition Careers
Occupational Therapy Careers
Office Occupations
Opticianry
Optometry
Packaging Science
Paralegal Careers
Paramedical Careers
Part-time & Summer Jobs
Performing Arts Careers
Petroleum Careers
Pharmacy Careers
Photography
Physical Therapy Careers
Physician Careers
Plastics Careers
Plumbing & Pipe Fitting
Podiatric Medicine
Printing Careers
Property Management Careers
Psychiatry
Psychology
Public Health Careers
Public Relations Careers
Purchasing Careers
Real Estate
Recreation and Leisure
Refrigeration and Air Conditioning
Religious Service
Restaurant Careers
Retailing
Robotics Careers
Sales Careers
Sales & Marketing
Secretarial Careers
Securities Industry
Social Science Careers
Social Work Careers
Speech-Language Pathology Careers
Sports & Athletics
Sports Medicine
State and Local Government
Teaching Careers
Technical Communications
Telecommunications
Television and Video Careers

Theatrical Design & Production
Transportation Careers
Travel Careers
Trucking Careers
Veterinary Medicine Careers
Vocational and Technical Careers
Welding Careers
Word Processing
Writing Careers
Your Own Service Business

CAREERS IN
Accounting; Advertising; Business; Communications; Computers; Education; Engineering; Health Care; Law; Marketing; Science

CAREER DIRECTORIES
Careers Encyclopedia
Occupational Outlook Handbook

CAREER PLANNING
Admissions Guide to Selective Business Schools
Career Planning and Development for College Students and Recent Graduates
Careers Checklists
Careers for Animal Lovers
Careers for Bookworms
Careers for Foreign Language Aficionados
Careers for Good Samaritans
Careers for Sport Nuts
Careers for Travel Buffs
Guide to Basic Resume Writing
Handbook of Business and Management Careers
Handbook of Scientific and Technical Careers
How to Change Your Career
How to Choose the Right Career
How to Get and Get Ahead On Your First Job
How to Get People to Do Things Your Way
How to Have a Winning Job Interview
How to Land a Better Job
How to Make the Right Career Moves
How to Prepare for College
How to Run Your Own Home Business
How to Succeed in High School
How to Write a Winning Resume
Joyce Lain Kennedy's Career Book
Life Plan
Planning Your Career of Tomorrow
Planning Your College Education
Planning Your Military Career
Planning Your Young Child's Education
Resumes for Communications Careers
Resumes for High Tech Careers
Resumes for Sales and Marketing Careers

SURVIVAL GUIDES
Dropping Out or Hanging In
High School Survival Guide
College Survival Guide

VGM Career Horizons
a division of *NTC Publishing Group*
4255 West Touhy Avenue
Lincolnwood, Illinois 60646-1975